TEACHER'S BOOK

Reading & Writing 1
TARGETS

Virginia Evans - Jenny Dooley

Express Publishing

Published in 1999 by Express Publishing

Liberty House New Greenham ParNewbury Berkshire RG19 6HW
Tel.: (0044) 1635 817 363 Fax: (0044) 1635 817 463
e-mail: inquiries@expresspublishing.co.uk
http: //www.expresspublishing.co.uk

© Virginia Evans - Jenny Dooley

Design & Illustration © Express Publishing

ISBN 1-903128-83-8

Contents

Abbreviations used in the book

e.g.	=	example
etc	=	et cetera
Ex	=	exercise
HW	=	homework
i.e.	=	that is
p	=	page
pp	=	pages
S	=	student
Ss	=	students
T	=	teacher

Introduction to the Teacher

Reading & Writing Targets 1, for learners of English at Elementary level, provides systematic development of students' reading and writing skills.

The book consists of 15 units and is planned to be taught in 20 - 25 teaching hours. The topics of the units have been carefully selected to appeal to and motivate learners at Elementary level. Each unit begins with a text, based on a real-life communicative situation, which not only develops reading skills but also serves as a model for the students' own written work.

A variety of reading skills — skimming for overall understanding, scanning, predicting a topic from visual prompts or clues, reconstructing a text, inferring, recognising word equivalences, jigsaw reading, etc — are introduced, taught and practised to help learners read more effectively in English.

The exercises that follow are specially chosen to expand learners' passive and active vocabulary and feed them with ideas which can be used by learners in their writing projects. Grammar structures are also presented and practised in a meaningful context to help learners produce successful pieces of writing.

The text types presented in this book include **informal letters, articles, recipes, advertisements, postcards, film reviews** and **stories** through pictures. Useful **Writing Tip** boxes help learners understand the structure of each piece of writing. **Paragraph Plans** are also provided to give the students step-by-step guidance. These plans are intended to be used in class for discussion before learners write their own pieces. Teachers are advised to elicit, in class, the points which learners should include in their piece of writing and always to have some students complete the task orally in class before the exercise is assigned as written homework.

The **Photo File section** at the end of the Student's Book provides pictures which students can use to decorate their writing projects for Units 2, 3, 6, 7, 9, 10 and 12.

Unit 1 - Family Ties (pp. 4 - 7)

```
┌─────────────────────────┐
│       Objectives        │
└─────────────────────────┘
```

Vocabulary: the family; jobs; simple physical descriptions; numbers
Grammar: the verb *to be* (present simple); the verb *have got* (present simple); personal pronouns; possessive adjectives; the possessive case *'s*; abbreviations; capital letters; full stops; the conjunction *and*
Reading: scanning for specific information
Writing: a project on your family

1 *(Point out that Ss should label the people according to how they are related to Carl.)*

1	sister	3	brother
2	mother	4	father

(Check Ss' answers by prompting sentences.
e.g. T: Number 1 — Who is she?
*   S1: She is Carl's sister.)*

2 *(Ask individual Ss to answer the questions orally, helping where necessary.)*

(Suggested answer)

There are four people in my family. My mother's name is Susan. My father's name is William. My brother's name is Neil and my sister's name is Tanya.

3 *(Read each of the statements aloud and ask Ss to identify them as true or false. Ss should be advised to scan the texts quickly for the relevant information, rather than reading for complete understanding.)*

2 T   3 T   4 F   5 T   6 F   7 F   8 T

(Ask individual Ss to take turns in reading portions of the text aloud and explain/elicit the meaning of any unknown vocabulary.)

4 1 b   2 a   3 d   4 c

5 a) *(Complete the task orally with the class, explaining/eliciting the meaning of any unknown words. Explain that **cousin** applies to both males and females.)*

male	
uncle	father
brother	husband
grandfather	son
cousin	grandson

female	
mother	cousin
wife	granddaughter
daughter	aunt
sister	grandmother

b) *(Ask Ss to make pairs of words. Write their answers in a list on the board, as shown below. Ss should copy this list in their notebooks.)*

mother — father
aunt — uncle
sister — brother
granddaughter — grandson
grandmother — grandfather
wife — husband
daughter — son

6 *(Write the words **am, are, isn't** and **aren't** on the board. Complete the task orally with the class.)*

Affirmative	Negative	Interrogative
I am	I'm not	Am I?
you **are**	you aren't	Are you?
he she it } **is**	he she it } **isn't**	Is { he? she? it?
we you they } **are**	we you they } **aren't**	Are { we? you? they?

7 *(After Ss have done Ex. 7, ask them to count from 1 to 100, one after the other.)*

one	1	twenty-three	23
twelve	12	nineteen	19
thirty-six	36	twenty-five	25
ten	10	forty-four	44
twenty-nine	29	fifty-eight	58

STUDY TIP (p. 5)

*(Present the use of **This is ...** and explain/elicit the meaning of **introduce**.)*

8 *(Explain/Elicit the meaning of the words in the list, then complete one or two examples orally with the class before Ss complete the task in writing. Check Ss' answers around the class, then ask individual Ss to read their answers aloud.)*

2 *Kate/29*
job – policewoman
This is Kate. She is twenty-nine years old. She is a policewoman.

3 *Roy/23*
job – porter
This is Roy. He is twenty-three years old. He is a porter.

4 *Jack/36*
job – reporter
This is Jack. He is thirty-six years old. He is a reporter.

5 *Carlos/44*
job – chef
This is Carlos. He is forty-four years old. He is a chef.

6 *Sarah/25*
job – nurse
This is Sarah. She is twenty-five years old. She is a nurse.

9 *(Copy the table in the S's book onto the board. Ask Ss to supply the missing forms and write their answers in the appropriate spaces on the board. If desired, read each line of the table aloud for Ss to repeat as a choral drill.)*

Affirmative	Negative	Interrogative
I've got	I haven't got	Have I got?
you**'ve got**	you **haven't got**	**Have** you **got**?
he she } **'s got** it	he she } hasn't got it	**Has** he she got? it
we you } 've got they	we you } **haven't got** they	**Have** we you got? they

10 *(Allow Ss a minute or two to match the items, then check Ss' answers around the class. As an extension, ask Ss to make sentences practising personal pronouns and possessive adjectives. Use the prompts below.*
Jack - car [e.g. He is Jack. This is his car.]
Bob & Sally - house
Claire - ball   etc.)

I	→	my	
you	→	your	
he	→	his	
she	→	her	
it	→	its	
we	→	our	
you	→	your	
they	→	their	

11 *(Allow Ss a minute or two to complete the task, then check Ss' answers by asking individual Ss to read the sentences aloud.)*

1 I   2 She   3 our   4 their

12 *(Copy the table in the S's book onto the board. Explain/Elicit the meaning of any unknown words. Then, ask Ss to identify which box[es] each word belongs in, and write their answers in the appropriate box[es] on the board.)*

HEIGHT:	*tall*, short, big, small
BUILD:	slim, plump, big, small, well-built
HAIR:	black, short, long, red, brown, grey, fair
EYES:	green, big, small, brown, blue, grey

13 a) *(Present the example in the S's book to ensure that Ss understand the task. Ss correct the remaining false statements as a written exercise. Check Ss' answers around the class.)*

2 T
3 F   Mark isn't short and plump. He is tall and slim.
4 F   Don isn't slim and (he) hasn't got fair hair. He is plump and (he) has got black hair.

b) *(Prompt a number of individual Ss to give an oral description of a friend, as in the suggested answer below. If desired, Ss may then be asked to complete the task in writing.)*

(Suggested answer)

Gabriella is short and slim. She has got long black hair and brown eyes.

14 *(Check that Ss understand the task, then prompt Ss to make sentences.*
e.g. T: Harold
*   S1: Harold is his grandfather.*
If desired, Ss may then be asked to complete the task in writing.)

6

Mary is his sister. Ian is his brother. Harold is his grandfather. Rachel is his grandmother. George is his uncle. Sue is his aunt. David is his cousin.

(As further practice, Ss may be prompted to speak about various people from the family tree.
e.g. T: She is Sue. Who is George?
S1: George is her husband.)

15 *(Allow Ss three minutes to complete the task. Check Ss' answers around the class, then ask individual Ss to read the sentences aloud.)*

1	mother	5	daughter
2	cousin	6	sister
3	brother	7	uncle
4	grandfather	8	grandson

STUDY TIP (p. 7)

*(Present the use of **'s** and explain/elicit the meaning of **possessive**, **belongs to** and **are related**.)*

16
1	is	4	has
2	possessive	5	possessive
3	is	6	has

STUDY TIP (p. 7)

*(Present the use of capital letters, full stops and the conjunction **and**.)*

17 *(Complete the first two sentences orally with the class and write these corrected sentences on the board. Allow Ss five minutes to complete the remainder of the task in writing, then check Ss' answers around the class.)*

I am **H**enry. **I** am thirty-five years old and **I** am a gardener. **I** am tall and plump. **I** have got short fair hair and green eyes. **M**y wife's name is **M**artha. **S**he is thirty years old and she is a chef. **O**ur daughter's name is **J**essica and she is seven years old**.**

WRITING TIP (p. 7)

(Present the theory in the Writing Tip box, reminding Ss that we don't necessarily give all of the information listed. Ss should read the texts in Ex. 3 again to see how this theory has been applied.)

18 **a)** *(Complete the first sentence orally with the class, then allow Ss two or three minutes to complete the task in writing. Check Ss' answers around the class.)*

My name is Emma.
I am thirty-four years old.
I am a nurse.
I have got long brown hair and green eyes.

b) *(Check that Ss understand the table, then prompt individual Ss to make sentences, as in the answers below. If desired, Ss may then be asked to complete the task in writing.)*

... thirty-five years old and he is a reporter. He is tall and he has got short brown hair and brown eyes.

This is my daughter, Vicky. She is eleven years old. She has got long brown hair and brown eyes.

This is my son, Phil. He is eight years old. He has got very short fair hair and green eyes.

19 *(Check that Ss understand the task and that they know the relevant vocabulary, especially concerning their parents' jobs. Ask Ss to look at the texts in Ex. 3 again, and remind them they must also describe themselves. Assign the task as written HW. Ss should write approximately 25 words for each family member.)*

Unit 2 - Celebrities (pp. 8 - 11)

Objectives

Vocabulary: jobs; countries; nationalities; colours; physical descriptions; activities; character descriptions
Grammar: the verb *to be* (present simple); the verb *have got* (present simple); the verb *can* (present simple); the conjunctions *and* and *but*
Reading: scanning; reading for specific information; cloze test
Writing: an article about a famous person

1 *(Ask Ss to look at the pictures and explain the meaning of **celebrities** and **famous**. Read aloud the names of the people in the pictures, then the words in the list, explaining/eliciting meaning where necessary. Ss match the jobs to the pictures, and label each picture appropriately.)*

a singer   d ice-skater
b actor   e film director
c model

(If desired, Ss may ask and answer questions in open/closed pairs.
e.g. S1: Who is this in picture 'e'?
S2: He's Steven Spielberg.
S1: What's his job?
S2: He's a film director.)

2 *(Before Ss read the text, ask them to read the numbered sentences quickly. Explain/Elicit the meaning of any unknown words, then allow Ss three or four minutes to read the text silently and underline the correct word in each sentence. Check Ss' answers by asking Ss to read the sentences aloud.)*

1	American	4	hardworking
2	father's	5	tennis
3	fair	6	purple

(Explain/Elicit the meaning of any words in the text which Ss still do not understand, then ask individual Ss to read portions of the text aloud.)

STUDY TIP (p. 9)

*(Present the theory about the verb **to be** and check that Ss understand the meaning of **nationality, appearance** and **character**.)*

3 **a)** *(Allow Ss about two minutes to complete the task. Check Ss' answers by reading aloud the name of each country. Ss respond, chorally or individually, by saying the appropriate nationality. Correct Ss' pronunciation where necessary and check that Ss understand the names of the countries in English.)*

2	h	4	e	6	g	8	f
3	a	5	b	7	c		

b) *(Read aloud each of the names in the key, then prompt Ss to respond chorally or individually, as in the example below. Point out that **Carlos, Edward** and **Hassan** are male names.*
e.g. T: Marie
S1: She's French.
Then, Ss ask and answer questions in open/closed pairs.)

SA: Is Edward Turkish?
SB: No, he isn't. He's English. Is Anouska French?

SA: No, she isn't. She's Finnish. Is Renata Greek?
SB: No, she isn't. She's Polish. Is Eleni English?
SA: No, she isn't. She's Greek. Is Gabriella Italian?
SB: Yes, she is. Is Hassan Polish?
SA: No, he isn't. He's Turkish.

STUDY TIP (p. 9)

*(Present the theory about **have/has got** and check that Ss know/remember the meaning of **possession** and **physical features**.)*

4 **a)** *(Read each colour aloud. Ss give the appropriate number and label the balloons accordingly. Then, read out the numbers at random, to which Ss respond by saying the colour, chorally or individually.)*

2	red	5	white	8	brown
3	orange	6	pink	9	black
4	green	7	yellow	10	purple

b) *(Ss ask and answer questions about each other's favourite colour, in open/closed pairs.)*

5 *(Allow Ss about two minutes to complete the task. Check Ss' answers by asking individual Ss to read their answers aloud.)*

(Suggested answers)

Tom is tall and plump. He has got **short brown wavy** hair and brown **eyes**. He has also got a beard and **a moustache**.
Anne is tall and slim. She **has got long fair** hair and green **eyes**.

6 *(Help individual Ss to complete the task orally. If desired, Ss may then repeat the task as a written exercise.)*

(Suggested answer)

Tara Lipinski is short and slim. She has got long fair hair and big blue eyes.

STUDY TIP (p. 10)

*(Present the use of **can**, and explain/elicit the meaning of any unknown words in the theory box.)*

7 *(Read each of the activities aloud. Ss identify the appropriate picture and label the pictures accordingly.)*

1	g	3	e	5	d	7	a
2	b	4	h	6	f	8	c

(Ask individual Ss around the class to say which things they can/can't do. If desired, Ss may then repeat the task as a written exercise.)

(Suggested answers)

I can swim.	I can't sing.
I can ride a bicycle.	I can't cook.
I can play tennis.	I can't windsurf.

STUDY TIP (p. 10)

*(Present the use of **and** and **but** and explain/elicit the meaning of any unknown words.)*

8 *(Present the examples given in the S's book, and point out that **Thomas** is a male name, while **Chris** is usually a male name but may also be used as a female name. Allow Ss two or three minutes to complete the task in writing. Check Ss' answers around the class, then ask individual Ss to read the completed sentences aloud.)*

3 Emily can't ride a bicycle but she can paint.
4 Thomas can windsurf and play tennis.
5 Anna can paint and cook.
6 Chris can sing but he/she can't ride a bicycle.

9 **a)** *(Read aloud each of the words in the list, explaining/eliciting their meaning where necessary. Ss label the pictures appropriately. Check Ss' answers by asking individual Ss to read the completed sentences aloud.)*

A	pilot	D	mechanics
B	clowns	E	photographer
C	artist	F	guitarist

b) *(Read each of the sentences aloud, and explain/elicit the meaning of any unknown words. Ss label the sentences appropriately. Check Ss' answers by asking individual Ss to make sentences, as in the answers below. If desired, Ss may then repeat the task as a written exercise.)*

2 C Artists can paint beautiful pictures.
3 F Guitarists can play the guitar very well.
4 D Mechanics can fix cars.
5 E Photographers can take good photographs.
6 A Pilots can fly planes.

10 *(Before Ss read the text, read aloud the clues below the crossword, and explain/elicit the meaning of any unknown words. Allow Ss five or six minutes to read the text silently and complete the*

crossword with the words missing from the clues. Check Ss' answers by asking individual Ss to read each of the completed clues aloud, and write the completed crossword on the board. Finally, ask individual Ss to read the text aloud.)*

Across

3	friendly	5	clever	6	kind

Down

1	hardworking	2	shy	4	lazy

11 *(Explain/Elicit the meaning of any unknown words. Ss then underline the appropriate adjectives. Check Ss' answers around the class.)*

shy, hardworking, clever, kind, friendly, lazy

(Ask individual Ss to make sentences, as in the answers below.)

(Suggested answers)

My mother is kind.
My big brother is hardworking.
My big sister is lazy.
My little brother is shy.
My little sister is friendly.

12 *(Complete the first sentence orally with the class. Ss then complete the task as a written exercise. Check Ss' answers around the class.)*

1 John can dance but he can't sing.
2 Liz has got long brown hair and blue eyes.
3 My favourite singer is Sting.

WRITING TIP (p. 11)

(Present the theory about writing an article about a person and explain/elicit the meaning of any unknown words.)

13 **a)** *(Check that Ss understand the task, and complete one or two examples orally with the class. Allow Ss three or four minutes to complete the task, then check Ss' answers around the class. Finally, ask individual Ss to read portions of the completed text aloud.)*

1	singer	5	slim	9	dance
2	father's	6	blue	10	favourite
3	mother's	7	fair		
4	brother	8	friendly		

b) *(Explain/Elicit the meaning of any unknown words. Ss then complete the task. Check Ss' answers around the class.)*

1 The first paragraph.
2 The fourth paragraph.
3 The third paragraph.
4 The second paragraph.

14 *(Point out to Ss that the paragraph plan given is the same as is illustrated in the text in Ex. 13. Ask Ss to read the information in the plan silently, then ask questions.*
e.g. T: *What's his name?*
S1: *Nicolas Cage.*
T: *What is his nationality?*
S2: *American.*
T: *Which year was he born?*
S3: *1964*
T: *What's his father's name?   etc.*
*Then, prompt individual Ss to complete the task orally, reminding them to use the text in Ex. 13 as a model and to use **and**/**but** where appropriate. Finally, assign the task as written HW.)*

(Suggested answer)

Nicolas Cage is a famous American actor. He was born in 1964.

His father's name is August and his mother's name is Joy. Nicolas has got two brothers. Their names are Marc and Christopher.

Nicolas is tall and slim. He has got short brown hair and green eyes. He is a kind, hardworking person.

Nicolas can paint but he can't play football. His favourite singer is Elvis Presley and his favourite colour is purple.

3 - Join the Club! (pp. 12 - 15)

```
┌─────────── Objectives ───────────┐
```

Vocabulary: sports; sports equipment
Grammar: *there is/are*; prepositions of place; commas; question marks
Reading: reading for specific information; scanning
Writing: an advertisement for a sports centre

1 *(Read items 1 - 8 aloud, and ask Ss to match these to the pictures. Ensure that Ss now understand the vocabulary in the exercise, and have grasped the dis-*

tinction between [e.g.] **tennis** *as a sport and* **tennis court** *as the place where the sport is played. If desired, allow Ss two or three minutes to memorise the items, then ask them to close their books. Point to each of the pictures; Ss identify the activities in each picture, chorally or individually.)*

1	H	3	G	5	D	7	F
2	A	4	B	6	C	8	E

2 *(Ensure that Ss are aware of the meaning of* **summer camp***: a residential centre where children/teenagers spend a summer holiday, and which offers sporting/ adventure activities supervised by young members of staff. Read aloud each of the statements below the text, and explain/elicit the meaning of any unknown words. Allow Ss five minutes to read the text silently and mark the statements as true or false. Check Ss' answers, then explain/elicit the meaning of any words in the text which Ss still do not understand. Finally, ask individual Ss to read the text aloud.)*

1 F	2 T	3 T	4 F	5 F	6 T

3 *(Allow Ss one or two minutes to match the adjectives to their opposites. Check Ss' answers. Ask Ss to find and underline the adjectives in the text. Emphasise that they should scan the text rapidly rather than reading each word. Then, help Ss identify the noun to which each adjective refers.)*

1	C	(children)	4	E	(staff)
2	A	(staff)	5	D	(countryside)
3	B	(staff)			

4 *(Read aloud the names of each of the items 1-10; Ss match these to the sports, labelling each sport appropriately in their books. If desired, point out that each sport is uncountable: thus* **a basketball** *is the equipment, but the game is* **basketball***;* **darts** *are equipment, but* **darts** *is a game.)*

cycling	3	skiing	9
table tennis	5	cricket	8
golf	1	ten-pin bowling	7
basketball	2	darts	10
canoeing	4		

5 *(Write the words* **play** *and* **go** *on the board, and ask Ss to guess which word is used with each of the sports in Ex. 4. Write each correct answer on the board, while Ss fill in the diagram in their books.)*

play: table tennis, golf, basketball, cricket, darts
go: swimming, cycling, canoeing, skiing, ten-pin bowling

6 *(Prompt individual Ss to make sentences orally. If desired, Ss may then repeat the task as a written exercise. Alternatively, Ss may be asked to close their books and make sentences from memory.)*

To go cycling you need a bicycle.
To play table tennis you need table tennis bats.
To play golf you need golf clubs.
To play basketball you need a basketball.
To go canoeing you need a canoe.
To go skiing you need skis.
To play cricket you need a cricket bat.
To go ten-pin bowling you need bowling pins.
To play darts you need darts.

7 *(Allow Ss one or two minutes to match the locations to the sports, then check Ss' answers by asking individual Ss to make sentences orally. If desired, Ss may then repeat the task as a written exercise.)*

2 F   3 C   4 A   5 G   6 E   7 B

You can play tennis on a tennis court.
You can go swimming in a swimming pool.
You can play golf on a golf course.
You can play cricket on a cricket pitch.
You can play football on a football pitch.
You can go ten-pin bowling at a bowling alley.

8 *(Allow Ss about five minutes to refer to the text in Ex. 2 again and complete the task. Check Ss' answers around the class.)*

1	hour's	5	beautiful
2	games	6	basketball
3	adventure	7	keep
4	main	8	summer

STUDY TIP (p. 14)

(Present the table and notes in the Study Tip box. If desired, ask Ss to make sentences about the sports equipment shown in Ex. 4, as in the examples below.
e.g.   SA: There is a bicycle.
SB: There are three darts.)

9 *(Allow Ss two or three minutes to complete the task. Check Ss' answers by asking individual Ss to read the complete sentences aloud.)*

2	There are	7	There is
3	There is	8	There are
4	There are	9	There is
5	There is	10	There are
6	There is		

Prepositions of Place (p. 14)

(Present the prepositions of place, reading each item aloud and ensuring that Ss understand the meaning of each.)

10 *(Ask Ss to look at the map, and check that they understand **cafeteria**. Complete the first two sentences orally with the class. Ss then complete the remainder of the task. Check Ss' answers around the class.)*

1 T   2 F   3 F   4 T   5 F

2   There is a football pitch **behind** the tennis courts.
3   There is a bowling alley **between** the swimming pool and the tennis courts.
5   The Super Sports Centre is **opposite** the bus station.

11 *(Ss ask and answer questions, first in open pairs, then in closed pairs. Monitor Ss' performance around the class.)*

(Suggested answers)

SA: Is there a football pitch at the Super Sports Centre?
SB: Yes, there is.
SA: Where is it?
SB: It's behind the tennis courts.
SA: Is there a bowling alley at the Super Sports Centre?
SB: Yes, there is.
SA: Where is it?
SB: It's between the swimming pool and the tennis courts.

STUDY TIP (p. 15)

(Present the use of commas and question marks and, if appropriate/possible, explain to Ss the difference in the use of these punctuation marks in English and in the Ss' mother tongue.)

12 *(Allow Ss a minute or two to complete the task, then check Ss' answers around the class.)*

... to send your children to in the summer holidays**?** Why don't you try Sunrise Summer Camp**?**

11

... All of the staff are experienced, energetic and, above all, enthusiastic ... there is a games room with snooker, table tennis and many other games ... For real adventure lovers, we have got water-skiing, canoeing and mountain biking ... For more information, call 888341...

13 *(Remind Ss that unless a sentence ends with a question mark [or exclamation mark], we must use a full stop at the end of each sentence. Point out that we do not use both together. Complete the first two items orally with the class, then allow Ss about two minutes to complete the remainder of the task on their own. Check Ss' answers around the class. Note: Tell Ss that we usually use a comma before **but** − especially in longer sentences.)*

1 Is there a swimming pool at the club**?**
2 There is a games room**.** There is also a café**.**
3 You can play football**,** tennis and cricket there**.**
4 Can we go canoeing at the camp**?**
5 There are two swimming pools and a bowling alley**,** but there isn't a tennis court**.**
6 Your children can do many activities there**,** such as canoeing, water-skiing and mountain biking**.**
7 The staff are friendly and experienced**.**
8 Has the centre got a basketball court**?**

14 *(If desired, briefly revise the theory in the Study Tip box at the bottom of p. 10. Present the example in the S's book, then allow Ss two or three minutes to complete the task. Check Ss' answers around the class.)*

2 You can play snooker **and** table tennis.
3 There are two swimming pools, **but** there aren't any tennis courts.
4 You can't play football, **but** you can go swimming.
5 The centre has got a café **and** a games room.

WRITING TIP (p. 15)

(Present the theory in the Writing Tip box and explain/elicit the meaning of any unknown words.)

15 *(Ask Ss to look at the advertisement and the plan below it. Help individual Ss to complete the task orally. Ask questions and elicit answers from Ss.*
T: *Where is the Mega Sports Centre?*
S1: *It's opposite the Grand Hotel on King Street.*
T: *Are the staff friendly?*
S2: *Yes, they are.*
T: *Are there any basketball courts at the centre?*
S3: *Yes, there are. There are two basketball courts.*

T: *What can you do on the basketball courts?*
S4: *You can play basketball. etc.*
After Ss have completed the task orally, assign it as written HW. Point out that Ss should use the opening and closing paragraphs given in the plan.)

(Suggested answer)

The Mega Sports Centre is the best sports centre in town. It's now open and, believe us, it's got something for everyone!

The Mega Sports Centre is opposite the Grand Hotel on King Street. We have got friendly, experienced staff and lots of sports and activities for everyone. There is a bowling alley, two basketball courts and two swimming pools. You can also play snooker, table tennis and darts in the Mega Sports Centre's huge games room. There is also the Mega Café − a great place to relax at the end of the day.

For more information, you can call us on 8825442.

Unit 4 - Seasons Change (pp. 16 - 19)

Objectives

Vocabulary: seasons; weather; activities/ events related to the different seasons
Grammar: present simple; prepositions of time; adverbs of frequency
Reading: reading for specific information; reading for gist
Writing: an article about your favourite season

1 *(Read aloud the names of the seasons and help Ss to match them to the pictures. Then, point to the pictures at random; Ss respond chorally by saying the name of the season.)*

spring   - B   autumn - A
summer - D   winter   - C

2 *(Read each of the sentences aloud and ask Ss to identify the season described. Then, explain/elicit the meaning of any unknown words, and ask individual Ss to read the sentences aloud.)*

1 winter   3 autumn
2 summer   4 spring

3 *(Explain/Elicit the meaning of any unknown words in the instructions, and check that Ss have understood the context of the passage. Then, read aloud the sentences following the text, explaining/ eliciting any unknown words. Allow Ss three or four minutes to read the text and mark the sentences as true or false. Check Ss' answers and explain/elicit the meaning of any words which Ss still do not understand.)*

1 F   2 F   3 T   4 T   5 F

4 *(Complete the task orally with the class, reminding Ss that they should 'skim' each paragraph rather than re-read the text in detail.)*

c   The first paragraph.
a   The second paragraph.
d   The third paragraph.
b   The fourth paragraph.

5 *(Write the names of the seasons on the board, and complete the table using Ss' oral answers. [Since seasons vary from country to country, the key here is only a suggested answer, showing the months and seasons in most European countries.] If desired, conduct a choral drill by reading aloud the months and/or seasons for Ss to repeat.)*

Winter: December, January, February
Spring: March, April, May
Summer: June, July, August
Autumn: September, October, November

6 *(Read the words [1-6] aloud and ask Ss to match each to its definition/synonym. Then, choose items at random from A to F; Ss respond by giving the matching word.)*

1 D   3 F/A   5 C
2 B   4 A/F   6 E

7 *(Allow Ss two or three minutes to complete the task. Check Ss' answers around the class.)*

1 build   3 ride   5 picnics
2 turns   4 feel   6 spend

8 a) *(Read aloud each of the activities [1-8], explaining/eliciting the meaning of any unknown words, and ask Ss to identify the appropriate season. [The suggested answers below would apply in many European countries; in other parts of the world, correct responses might be markedly different.])*

(Suggested answers)

1 S   3 W   5 S   7 W
2 A   4 SP   6 A   8 SP/S

b) *(Write the seasons on the board and prompt Ss to suggest further activities associated with each. Help Ss with vocabulary if necessary, and complete the table on the board using Ss' suggestions.)*

WINTER:	play in the snow, sit by the fire, etc
SPRING:	fly kites, go for walks, etc
SUMMER:	school finishes, go swimming, eat ice cream, etc
AUTUMN:	collect wood for the fire, go shopping for new warm clothes, etc

c) *(Ask individual Ss to make sentences orally, then assign the task as a written exercise. Check Ss' answers around the class.)*

(Suggested answers)

In the winter, I play in the snow with my brother.
In the spring, I go for walks with my family.
In the spring, I go on picnics.
In the summer, I go swimming.
In the summer, I go on holiday.
In the autumn, I go shopping for new warm clothes with my mother.
In the autumn, I collect the leaves from the garden.

9 *(Write the prepositions on the board, then read aloud each item from the list in the S's book. Ask Ss to identify the word used with each preposition and use Ss' answers to complete the table on the board. Ss fill in the table in their books.)*

IN	*the morning, August, May, the summer, the evening, July, the autumn, the afternoon*
AT	*noon, midnight, the weekend, 10 o'clock*
ON	*Wednesday, Saturday, Tuesday*

10 *(Read aloud the adjectives in the list, explaining/ eliciting the meaning of any unknown words. Allow Ss about three minutes to complete the task, then check Ss' answers by asking individual Ss to read the completed descriptions aloud.)*

2 warm   4 hot, sunny
3 cool   5 rainy, windy

STUDY TIP (p. 18)

(Present the theory about adverbs of frequency and explain/elicit the meaning of any unknown words. If desired, use the chart in Ex. 11 to clarify the meaning of each adverb of frequency.)

11 *(Invite a number of Ss to complete the sentences orally; Ss then repeat the task as a written exercise. Check Ss' answers around the class.)*

(Suggested answers)

1 I **always** feel happy in the spring.
2 My family and I **sometimes** go on holiday in the summer.
3 I **never** go skiing in the summer.
4 We **often** visit our grandparents at the weekend.
5 I **never** go on picnics in the winter.

12 *(If necessary, point out to Ss that the weather described is that of many European countries. Complete the task orally with the class, then ask individual Ss to read the completed text aloud.)*

2 cloudy   4 snows   6 sunny
3 rains   5 hot   7 windy

(If desired/applicable, Ss may be prompted to give a similar short oral/written description of winter and summer in their country.)

13 *(Explain/Elicit the meaning of any of the words in bold which Ss do not know/remember. Allow Ss about five minutes to read the passage and complete the task. Check Ss' answers around the class, then ask individual Ss to read the completed text aloud.)*

1 change   5 fly   9 help
2 rains   6 buys   10 visit
3 blows   7 starts   11 like
4 fall   8 collects   12 makes

WRITING TIP (p. 19)

(Present the theory in the Writing Tip box, and explain/elicit the meaning of any unknown words.)

14 a) *(Ensure that Ss understand the context of the passage and the nature of the task. Emphasise that Ss should not read the text in detail at this stage, but should 'skim' to find the main topic of*

each paragraph, and number this according to the theory in the Writing Tip box. If necessary, help Ss complete the task.)

A 3   B 1   C 4   D 2

b) *(Complete the task orally with the class.)*

1 season   3 activities
2 nature   4 feelings

(Finally, explain/elicit the meaning of any words which Ss still do not understand, then ask individual Ss to read portions of the text aloud in the correct order.)

15 *(Explain that Ss should write a piece similar to the texts in Exs 3 and 14 and should follow the plan in the S's book. [If the prompts provided in the S's book do not apply to the climate of the Ss' country, help Ss to suggest suitable prompts of their own and write these on the board.] Remind Ss that they do not need to use all of the prompts given. Ask individual Ss to complete the task orally by asking questions using the prompts.*
e.g. T: Why is summer your favourite season?
*   S1: Because it's beautiful.*
*   T: What's the weather like?*
*   S2: It's hot and sunny. The sun shines. There aren't any clouds. etc.*
After Ss have completed the task orally, assign it as written HW.)

(Suggested answer)

Summer is Great!

Summer is a fantastic season. It's my favourite because everything is so beautiful.

The weather is usually hot and sunny. The sun shines and there aren't any clouds. The trees are full of green leaves, the birds sing and the sea is warm.

In summer, I always go on holiday. In the morning, I swim in the sea and make sandcastles on the beach. In the afternoon, I go on picnics or ride my bicycle.

I love summer. It makes me feel happy and relaxed.

Unit 5 - Time Off (pp. 20 - 23)

Objectives

Vocabulary: holiday activities; likes/dislikes; adjectives describing a place
Grammar: present continuous; reflexive pronouns
Reading: reading for specific information
Writing: a postcard to a friend from a holiday resort

1 *(Explain/Elicit the meaning of the title of the unit and point out that the pictures show places related to relaxation, holidays, etc. Read aloud each of items 1 - 7 and ask Ss to match these to the photographs. Ensure that Ss now understand the vocabulary in the exercise by asking them to explain each item in their mother tongue. Additionally/Alternatively, allow Ss two or three minutes to memorise the vocabulary before closing their books. Point to each of the pictures. Ss respond, chorally or individually, by giving the English word for each place shown.)*

1 D   2 C   3 B   4 F   5 A   6 G   7 E

2 *(Explain/Elicit that the postcards are written to friends in England by a person on holiday on Capri, Italy, and another person on holiday in Jasper National Park in the Canadian Rockies. Explain/Elicit briefly where each place is. Ask Ss to read the questions first, then allow them four or five minutes to read the postcards and prepare their answers. Check Ss' answers around the class, then ask individual Ss to read portions of the postcards aloud.)*

1 Ben is on Capri.
2 He is staying at a lovely hotel in the Marina Grande.
3 It is sunny.
4 The food is very tasty.
5 Kate is staying at a big campsite in Jasper National Park (in the Canadian Rockies).
6 She is having breakfast at the campsite café.
7 Yes, she does.
8 The postcards start with "Dear Emily," and "Dear Michael," and end with "Love, Ben" and "Yours, Kate".

3 *(Allow Ss three or four minutes to scan the texts in Ex. 2 and complete the task. Check Ss' answers around the class.)*

1 fresh   5 beaches
2 square   6 tasty
3 sunny   7 morning
4 have   8 breakfast

STUDY TIP (p. 21)

*(Present the use of the present continuous and explain/elicit the meaning of any unknown words. Point out that **right now** is usually reserved for actions happening around the time of speaking. Remind Ss of the spelling rules which apply when forming the present continuous:*

Spelling Rules
- *Most verbs: add -ing after the base form of the main verb. e.g. read - **reading***
- *Verbs ending in one stressed vowel and a consonant: double the consonant and add -ing. e.g. swim - **swimming***
- *Verbs ending in -e: drop the e and add -ing. e.g. make - **making**)*

4 a) *(Present the example in the S's book, then allow Ss four or five minutes to complete the task. Monitor Ss' performance around the class, then ask individual Ss to read the completed sentences aloud. Write each of the verbs on the board, in both the infinitive and the present continuous forms, and draw Ss' attention to the spelling rules governing the present continuous, as above.)*

2 Mark is exploring the forest.
3 Jane is making a sandcastle now.
4 She is taking photos of the castle.
5 They are buying souvenirs at the moment.
6 My sister is sunbathing and I am writing postcards.
7 They are having coffee at a café.

b) *(Allow Ss about a minute to complete the task. Check Ss' answers by asking them to read aloud the sentence relevant to each photograph.)*

A 4   B 5   C 7   D 1

5 *(Read aloud each of the items in the list and ask Ss to identify the relevant picture. Ask Ss to make sentences orally, then assign as written HW.)*

(Suggested answers)

2 They are buying souvenirs.
3 They are eating watermelon.
4 They are sunbathing.
5 She is windsurfing.

15

6   They are ice-skating.
7   He is reading a book.
8   They are having lunch.
9   He is swimming.
10   She is playing volleyball.

6 *(Draw Ss' attention to the sentence **I'm really enjoying myself** in the last paragraph of Ben's post-card on p. 20. If necessary, briefly present the use of reflexive pronouns. Allow Ss two or three minutes to complete the task, then check Ss' answers by asking them to read the completed table aloud, chorally or individually.)*

You're enjoying yourself.
She's enjoying herself.
It's enjoying itself.
You're enjoying yourselves.
They're enjoying themselves.

STUDY TIP (p. 22)

*(Present the theory in the Study Tip box and explain/elicit the meaning of any unknown words. [Note that **think** in this context means "have the opinion that".] Point out that these verbs refer to a state of mind rather than an action.)*

7 *(Complete the first one or two extracts orally with the class, then allow Ss three or four minutes to complete the remainder of the task on their own. Monitor Ss' performance around the class, and check Ss' answers by asking individual Ss to read the completed extracts aloud.)*

1   am having, am staying
2   is swimming, is visiting
3   like, hate
4   are enjoying, think
5   is, am sunbathing, are making
6   is windsurfing, goes, are having

8 *(Complete the first sentence orally with the class, then allow Ss two or three minutes to complete the task in writing. Check Ss' answers by asking Ss to read the completed sentences aloud. After each sentence is read aloud, ask Ss to identify and label the appropriate picture.)*

1   are having   5   are eating
2   is fishing   6   is throwing
3   are sailing   7   are having
4   is visiting

A 7   C 2   E 3   G 4
B 5   D 1   F 6

9 **a)** *(Without explaining the meaning of the words in bold, read each extract aloud and ask Ss to complete the task. Point out that these extracts are people's impressions of the place where they are.)*

1   Amy and Greg (A & C)
2   Peggy and Ross (B & D)

b) *(Read aloud each of the adjectives in the list using vocal intonation to help Ss identify whether each is positive or pejorative. Then, ask individual Ss to read the extracts aloud, with suitable substitutions.)*

(Suggested answers)

A beautiful   C wonderful
B disgusting/horrible D horrible/disgusting

10 *(Complete the first two sentences orally with the class, then allow Ss five or six minutes to complete the remainder of the task in writing. Monitor Ss' performance around the class. Check Ss' answers by asking individual Ss to read the complete sentences aloud. Write their answers on the board.)*

Dear Joe,
    I am having a wonderful time in Malta. We are staying at a lovely hotel in Valletta.
    It is warm and sunny today. Right now, I am sunbathing on the beach and [I am] writing this postcard. Jill is visiting a museum and Diane is having breakfast at a café. The water here is very blue and the beach is beautiful.
    We are really enjoying ourselves! I think Malta is a fantastic island.
                        Love,
                        Laura

(Read each of the questions aloud and invite Ss to respond.)

1   The postcard is from Laura.
2   The postcard is to Joe.
3   The postcard starts with "Dear Joe," and it ends with "Love, Laura".
4   The second paragraph is about the weather and what everyone is doing.
5   The last/third paragraph is about Laura's impressions of the place.

WRITING TIP (p. 23)

*(Present the theory in the Writing Tip box and explain/elicit the meaning of **impressions**. Ask Ss to look briefly at the texts in Exs. 2 and 10 and confirm whether each postcard conforms to the theory presented.)*

11 *(Ask each S to remember/imagine a holiday destination and help them to suggest prompts relevant to each paragraph of the postcard. Write a variety of these prompts on the board.*

e.g. 1. <u>Where</u>: Sicily — Hawaii [etc]
        lovely hotel — beautiful
        campsite — friend's house
    2. <u>Weather</u>: warm and sunny — hot, sun
            shining — wonderful warm
            afternoon etc

Remind Ss that they are to write about one destination and should choose appropriate prompts. Help Ss to complete the task orally, then assign it as written HW. Point out that their writing should look like the postcards in Ex. 2.)

(Suggested answer)

Dear Julie,

We are having a lovely time here in Sicily. We are staying at a big hotel in Palermo.

The weather is very hot and the sun is shining. At the moment, I am sitting by the pool at the hotel. Jane is buying souvenirs and Sarah is eating an ice cream at a café. The countryside is beautiful and Palermo is very interesting.

I really love it here! I think Sicily is a wonderful island.

Love,
Celia

Unit 6 - What's Cooking? (pp. 24 - 27)

Objectives

Vocabulary: food, ways of cooking
Grammar: the imperative; plurals; uncountable nouns; *how much/how many; some/any*
Reading: reading for specific information; scanning
Writing: a recipe

*(Ask Ss to look at the pictures on p. 24. Read the heading **vegetables** aloud; Ss repeat the word,*

chorally and/or individually. Read aloud each of the items in the group; again, Ss repeat each item, chorally and/or individually. Repeat this procedure for the remaining groups.)

*(For **Exs 1 - 5**, read each of the questions aloud and invite Ss to respond orally.)*

1 **(Suggested answers)**

a) lettuce, tomato, ham, cucumber, eggs, cheese, mayonnaise, tomato ketchup, olive oil, salt, pepper, vinegar

b) eggs, butter, cheese, tomato, green pepper, ham, olives, onions, potato, bacon, salt, pepper

c) flour, milk, eggs, sugar, butter

d) bread, butter, tomato, cheese, lettuce, cucumber, ham, mayonnaise, bacon, eggs, salt, pepper, mustard, tomato ketchup

2 **(Suggested answer)**

Peaches are my favourite fruit.

3 **(Suggested answer)**

I like fruit salad and ice cream.

4 **(Suggested answer)**

My favourite drink is milk.

5 **(Suggested answers)**

a) omelette, pizza, fish & chips, soup, beef & beans, chicken & rice, sausages

b) chef's salad, sandwich, soup, sausages

c) soup, sausages

STUDY TIP (p. 25)

(Present the use of the imperative and explain/elicit the meaning of any unknown words.)

6 *(Read aloud each of the items in the list. Ss identify and label the relevant pictures. If desired, allow Ss three or four minutes to memorise as many of the items as possible, then ask them to close their books. Point to each of the pictures in the book and invite Ss to say the relevant phrase, chorally or individually.)*

2 peel the banana
3 add the sugar
4 beat the mixture
5 break the eggs into a bowl
6 mix all the ingredients well
7 slice the meat

8 pour the coffee
9 chop the onion

7 *(Read aloud the prompts below each picture and explain/elicit the meaning of the verbs and equipment, in Ss' mother tongue if necessary. Read aloud each of the types of food in the list. Ss identify the picture[s] relevant to each one and list the types of food in their books accordingly.)*

(Suggested answers)

1 *eggs*, potatoes, fish, rice
2 potatoes, cake, biscuits, fish, bread
3 fish, sausages
4 *eggs*, potatoes, fish, rice, bread, sausages

(Ask individual Ss to make sentences orally, using the prompts. If desired, Ss may then be asked to repeat the task as a written exercise [4 to 5 sentences].)

(Suggested answers)

1 You can boil rice in a saucepan.
2 You can bake a cake in an oven.
3 You can grill fish on a barbecue.
4 You can fry potatoes in a frying pan.

Plurals (p. 25)

(Present the table of plurals, reading each pair of items aloud. Ss repeat, chorally or individually. Draw Ss' attention to the spelling of the plural forms.)

8 *(Allow Ss two or three minutes to complete the task. Ask Ss to read their answers aloud and spell each plural correctly. Write these answers on the board.)*

1 cakes	4 tomatoes	7 onions	
2 cherries	5 peaches	8 carrots	
3 biscuits	6 loaves		

STUDY TIP (p. 26)

*(Present the theory in the Study Tip box and explain/elicit the meaning of **uncountable** [nouns which we cannot count – e.g. flour]. Ask Ss to look at the pictures below the Study Tip box. Read each of the phrases aloud. Ss repeat, chorally or individually. Finally, explain/elicit the meaning of any words which Ss still do not understand.)*

9 *(Complete the first two or three items orally with the class. Allow Ss two or three minutes to complete the remainder of the task on their own, and check Ss' answers by asking individual Ss to read aloud the correct phrases [e.g. a cup of tea - a cup of coffee].)*

(incorrect words)

2 beer	5 sugar	8 juice
3 coffee	6 soup	9 chicken
4 flour	7 wine	

10 a) *(Read aloud each of the verbs in the list and explain/elicit the meaning of any unknown words; also explain the meanings of the headings **Ingredients** and **Dressing**. Ask Ss to look at the instructions in the recipe, and complete the first three items orally with the class. Allow Ss about five minutes to complete the task, and check Ss' answers by asking individual Ss to read the completed instructions aloud.)*

1 Boil	4 Remove	7 Add
2 Cut	5 Put	8 pour
3 Slice	6 mix	9 Serve

b) *(Read each of the statements aloud and ask Ss to say whether they are true or false. Emphasise that Ss should scan the text quickly to find the relevant information, rather than reading the entire text again in detail. Ask individual Ss to correct the false statements and read the corrected statements aloud.)*

1 T	2 F	3 F	4 T	5 F

2 Boil the eggs for **10** minutes.
3 Cut the cheese and the ham into **small** pieces.
5 Serve with fresh **bread**.

STUDY TIP (p. 27)

*(Present the use of **how much** and **how many**. If desired, ask Ss to find examples from p. 24 of each sort of noun, and to form questions similar to those modelled in the Study Tip box.)*

11 *(Explain/Elicit the meaning of **supermarket, frozen pizza base** and **mushrooms** if necessary. Complete the first one or two examples orally with the class, then allow Ss two or three minutes to complete the remainder of the task on their own. Check Ss' answers, then ask Ss to read the dialogue aloud in open or closed pairs.)*

1 many	3 much	5 many
2 many	4 many	6 much

STUDY TIP (p. 27)

*(Present the use of **some** and **any**, reminding Ss of the meaning of **affirmative** and **negative** if necessary.)*

12 *(Explain/Elicit the meaning of **hungry** and **Mediterranean** and any other unknown vocabulary. Complete the first one or two examples orally with the class, then allow Ss two or three minutes to complete the remainder of the task on their own. Check Ss' answers, then ask Ss to read the dialogue aloud in open and/or closed pairs.)*

1 some	4 How much	7 any
2 how many	5 any	8 some
3 some	6 any	9 any

WRITING TIP (p. 27)

(Present the theory in the Writing Tip box. Ask Ss to look again at the recipe in Ex. 10 and to confirm whether it conforms to the theory presented here. [The recipe in Ex. 10 conforms to the theory, but contains additional information concerning the dressing.])

13 *(Ensure that Ss understand the task and the plan given in the S's book. Ask Ss to find the name of the dish mentioned in the dialogue in Ex. 10; write the title **Mediterranean Omelette** on the board. Then, write the heading **Ingredients** on the board and, below this, the quantities required.*
i.e.   Ingredients
          2 ...
          1 ...   etc
*Ask Ss to scan the dialogue in Ex. 12 and underline each of the ingredients mentioned. Write Ss' answers in the appropriate spaces on the board. Next, write the heading **Instructions** on the board. Ask Ss to find and number the instructions given in the dialogue. Help individual Ss to read the instructions aloud, in order, as shown below. Assign the task as written HW.)*

(Suggested answer)

Mediterranean Omelette

Ingredients

    2 eggs
    1 small onion
    1 small green pepper
    1 large tomato
    25g butter
    salt and pepper

Instructions

- Cut the onion, the green pepper and the tomato into small pieces.
- Put the butter into the frying pan.
- Put the vegetables into the frying pan.
- Fry them for about three minutes.
- Break the eggs into a bowl.
- Add the salt and pepper.
- Beat the eggs well.
- Add the eggs to the frying pan.
- Cook the omelette for three minutes.
- Turn the omelette over.
- Serve with fresh bread.

Unit 7 - A Day in the Life of ... (pp. 28 - 31)

Objectives

Vocabulary: daily routines/activities; free-time activities; telling the time
Grammar: the present simple
Reading: reading for specific information
Writing: an article about a famous person's daily routine

---

1 *(Ask Ss to look at the pictures and identify the person. Ss have seen the same person in Unit 2. Point out that Tara goes to the Detroit Skating Club to practise because she is an ice-skater. Note: Explain to Ss that **practise** is a verb whereas **practice** is a noun.)*

- Yes, I do. She's Tara Lipinski.
- She's a famous Olympic gold medallist ice-skater.

(Suggested answers)

- I think she gets up at 7:30 in the morning.
- I think she goes to the Detroit Skating Club at 8:30 in the morning.
- I think she has five hours of practice every day. Yes, I do.
- Yes, I do.

2 *(Ss read the text silently. Do not explain any unknown words to Ss, since this will be presented in Exs. 3, 4 and 5.)*

1 F	2 F	3 F	4 F	5 T	6 F

3 *(Ss close their books. Draw a clock face on the board and write **o'clock, half past, past, to, a quarter past** and **a quarter to** in the appropriate places.*

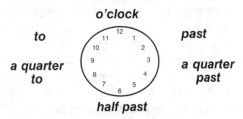

Draw hands on the clock face and practise telling the time with Ss.

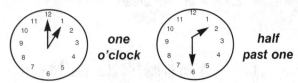

Ss open their books. Explain that we can tell the time in two ways. Ss look at the table in Ex. 3 on p.29 in their books. Explain the table to Ss, then play the game below or go straight on to the exercise.

Game

Divide the class into two teams. Write a time on the board. In teams, Ss tell the time in both ways. Each correct answer gets one point. The team with the most points is the winner.

T: *[T writes 8:30 on the board.]*
Team A S1: *Half past eight or eight thirty.*
T: *Very good. One point for Team A. Team B now.*
[T writes 9:00 on the board.]
Team B S1: *Nine o'clock or nine.*
T: *Well done.   etc)*

1   It's one o'clock. / It's one.
2   It's half past five. / It's five thirty.
3   It's a quarter past nine. / It's nine fifteen.
4   It's a quarter to six. / It's five forty-five.
5   It's ten to two. / It's one fifty.
6   It's twenty-five past one. / It's one twenty-five.

4 *(Ask Ss to look at the pictures, then scan the text of Ex. 2 and find the phrases which match the pictures. Do the first two examples with Ss orally, then Ss complete the rest of the exercise in closed pairs. Check Ss' answers around the class.)*

(Suggested answers)

- *Then,* at eight thirty, her mum drives her to the club.
- She practises from nine till lunchtime at twelve.

- *After that,* she has lunch till one.
- *Then,* from one till two forty-five she works with her coaches.
- At two forty-five, her mum drives her home.
- She has lessons at home from three till six thirty.
- *After that,* at six thirty, she makes dinner with her mum.
- They have dinner at seven thirty.
- *Then,* at eight, she does her homework or watches TV.
- *After that,* she has a shower at nine, *then* she goes to bed at nine thirty.

5 *(Explain any unknown words, then Ss do the exercise. Ask some Ss to talk about their daily routine. This can be assigned as written HW.)*

(Suggested answers)

MORNING

First, I get up at half past seven.
Next, I have a shower at twenty to eight.
Then, at eight o'clock, I get dressed.
At ten past eight, I have breakfast.
After that, I drive to work at half past eight.
Then, at nine o'clock, I start work.

AFTERNOON

I finish work at five o'clock.
After that, I go home at half past five.

EVENING

I cook dinner at seven o'clock.
Then, I have dinner at half past seven.
Next, I watch TV till nine o'clock.
After that, I go out till half past ten.
Then, I go to bed at eleven o'clock.

6 **(Suggested answers)**

I never go fishing in my free time.
I rarely watch TV in my free time.
I often go swimming in my free time.
I usually go to the cinema in my free time.
I sometimes go for a walk in my free time.
I rarely go on a picnic in my free time.
I sometimes go roller-skating in my free time.
I sometimes go shopping in my free time.
I usually read a book in my free time.
I always meet my friends in my free time.
I often go to a disco in my free time.
I rarely play computer games in my free time.

7 **(Suggested answers)**

I always meet my friends in my free time.
I usually go shopping.
I sometimes go to the cinema.
I often go to a restaurant.

(Read the table and explain the use of the present simple and the spelling rules. Drill your Ss. Say verbs in the first person singular. Ss say the same verbs in the third person singular.
e.g. *T:* *I play*
S1: he plays
T: *I swim*
S2: he swims
T: *I ride*
S3: he rides)

8 **a)** A 5   B 3   C 2   D 4   E 1

b) A: likes
B: has, teaches, stays, goes, prepares
C: gets up, has, catches, arrives, starts
D: helps, has, go, listen
E: works

c) Paragraph 1:   Who the person is and where he works.
Paragraph 2:   What Tim does in the morning.
Paragraph 3:   What Tim does in the afternoon.
Paragraph 4:   What Tim does in the evening.
Paragraph 5:   What Tim does in his free time.

9 *(Explain* **celebrity casting agent**, **am** *[=ante meridiem] and* **pm** *[=post meridiem] to Ss. Ask individual Ss to read aloud what Patty says and explain/elicit the meaning of any unknown words. Write these headings on the board:* **morning, afternoon, evening, free time**, *and fill in the information about Patty eliciting answers from Ss. Ss copy the table into their notebooks. Ask some Ss to talk about Patty's daily routine and free-time activities using their notes.*

morning - *get up (8:30)*
drive to work
arrive at work (10:00)
have breakfast (10:30)
read the newspaper
rarely/have lunch
afternoon - *have meetings with various celebrities (1:00 - 4:30)*
leave the office (5:00)

evening - *often/have dinner with a celebrity (6:30)*
sometimes/work late
get home (12:00)
free time - *meet friends*
go on a picnic)

(Suggested answers)

1   In the morning, Patty gets up at eight thirty. Then, she drives to work. She arrives at work at about ten o'clock. She has breakfast at work at half past ten and she also reads the newspaper. She rarely has lunch because she is very busy.

2   In the afternoon, Patty has meetings with various celebrities from one till four thirty. Patty usually leaves the office at about five o'clock.

3   In the evening, she often has dinner with a celebrity at about half past six. Sometimes she works late and doesn't get home till midnight.

4   In her free time, Patty meets her friends or goes on a picnic.

10 *(Ss use the completed table to write their articles.)*

(Suggested answer)

Patty Stevens is a celebrity casting agent at the Talent Corporation in London.

Patty's day starts early. First, she gets up at half past eight. Then, she drives to work. She usually arrives there at about ten o'clock. After that, she has breakfast at work at about half past ten. She also reads the newspaper. Patty rarely has lunch because she is busy.

At one o'clock, she has meetings with various celebrities till four thirty. She usually leaves the office at about five o'clock.

In the evening, she usually has dinner with a celebrity at about half past six. Sometimes she works late and doesn't get home till midnight.

In her free time, Patty meets her friends or goes on a picnic.

Unit 8 - What's the Story? (pp. 32 - 35)

Objectives

Vocabulary: emotions/reactions; adverbial phrases of time
Grammar: past simple; time links showing sequence *(later, before, after, when, etc)*
Reading: reading for detailed understanding; reading for gist
Writing: a story (3rd person)

1 *(Ask Ss to look at the pictures; read each of the phrases aloud, and help Ss to identify each of the things referred to. Ensure that Ss have clearly grasped the meaning of the new vocabulary [e.g. **military air base, parachute,** etc] and explain the meaning further if necessary. Then, point to various details [e.g. **parachute**] in the pictures and ask Ss to say chorally or individually, what each is called in English.)*

a) A & B   c) A & B   e) A
b) B & C   d) B & C

2 *(Read each of the items aloud, and prompt Ss to match them to the speech bubbles.)*

1 "Would you like some sugar?"
2 "Watch out!"
3 "I'm so sorry! My parachute didn't open on time!"
4 "I'm afraid there isn't any tea for you!"

3 *(Remind Ss of the use of the past simple tense, and revise/present the regular* **-ed** *ending. Read aloud each of the regular verbs in the table, in present and past form; Ss repeat, chorally and/or individually. Revise/Present the past tense of irregular verbs, reminding Ss that the past tense of* **be** *is* **was** *in the first/third person singular, but* **were** *in other persons. Read aloud each of the verbs. Ss repeat. Explain/ Elicit the meaning of any verbs in the table which Ss do not understand. Then, ask Ss to read the story and write each of the numbered verbs in the correct form. Point out that the story happened in the past ["last May"], and the events must therefore be narrated in the past tense. Complete the first paragraph orally with the class, then allow Ss five or six minutes to complete the remainder of the text on their own. Check Ss' answers around the class, then ask individual Ss to read the completed text aloud. Finally, explain/elicit the meaning of any vocabulary in the story which Ss still do not understand.)*

1	decided	7	landed	13	began
2	brought	8	fell	14	said
3	poured	9	looked	15	were
4	asked	10	was	16	came
5	could	11	said	17	had
6	heard	12	looked	18	sat

STUDY TIP (p. 33)

(Present the theory in the Study Tip box and explain/elicit the meaning of any unknown words.)

4 *(Explain that the events listed are in jumbled chronological order, and point out that the event at the end of the list actually occurs at the beginning of the story. Help Ss to number the second sentence correctly, then allow Ss about three minutes to complete the remainder of the task. Check Ss' answers around the class.)*

1 We decided to have tea in the garden.
2 Mum brought out biscuits, a cake and a pot of tea.
3 We heard a loud cry.
4 A soldier landed on the table.
5 We fell off our chairs.
6 We all began to laugh.
7 The soldier came back with a box of cakes.
8 We all had tea together in the dining room.

5 *(Before Ss complete the task, explain/elicit the meaning of the following vocabulary:* **pilot, air force, skating club, helicopter, [blow] - blew - [blown], umbrella, passed my driving test, anxiously.** *Ss then complete the task. Check Ss' answers by asking individual Ss to read the sentences aloud. If necessary, point out that* **watch** *implies paying attention to what one sees.)*

1 military air base   5 parachute
2 watch   6 Fortunately
3 pour   7 cheerfully
4 flew

STUDY TIP (p. 33)

(Present the theory in the Study Tip box. Ask Ss to read the first paragraph of the story in Ex. 2, then ask Ss questions.)

T: Where does the story take place?
S1: In the garden.
T: When does it take place?
S2: On a sunny afternoon last May.
T: Who are the people in the story?
S3: The writer, her mother and the soldier.

T: *What happened first?*
S4: *The writer's mother brought out biscuits, a cake and a pot of tea.)*

1	When	4	Later	7	Finally
2	First	5	After	8	before
3	Then	6	Next	9	After

6 *(Allow Ss about three minutes to complete the task, then check Ss' answers around the class.)*

1 b   2 a   3 b   4 b   5 a   6 b

7 *(Explain the nature of the task, and complete the first sentence orally with the class. Allow Ss about three minutes to complete the remainder of the task, then check Ss' answers by asking individual Ss to read the completed sentences aloud.)*

1 Last night I went to a restaurant.
2 I sat down at an empty table and waited for my friend.
3 Suddenly, a good-looking woman came towards my table.
4 "Who is she?" I wondered.

8 *(Explain to Ss that the paragraphs are in jumbled order, but that all the events took place in the past ["Last year" - Paragraph D] and must therefore be narrated in the past tense. Point out that if Ss do not know the past tense of a verb, they should consult the list of irregular verbs on p. 64; if the verb is not listed, they may assume that it has a regular **-ed** past form.)*

a) *(Complete Paragraph A orally with the class, helping Ss to use the list of verbs on p. 64. Allow Ss five or six minutes to complete the remainder of the task, then check Ss' answers around the class.)*

A put on, got, heard, thought
B laughed, said, pressed
C jumped, opened, was, ran, looked, asked
D went, stayed

b) *(Allow Ss a minute or two to determine the correct order of paragraphs; emphasize that Ss should "skim" each paragraph rather than re-reading each word carefully. Check Ss' answers, then ask individual Ss to read the story aloud in the correct chronological sequence.)*

A 2   B 4   C 3   D 1

9 *(Complete the first two sentences orally with the class, then allow Ss two or three minutes to complete the remainder of the task. Check Ss' answers by asking individual Ss to read the corrected sentences aloud. Finally, explain/elicit the meaning of any unknown words.)*

10 *(Read aloud the adverbial phrases in list A and the actions in list B, and explain/elicit the meaning of any unknown words. Point out that the adverbial phrases all refer to <u>when</u> an action took place <u>in the past</u>. If desired, ask the class to give the past tense of each verb, then ask several individual Ss to make sentences orally. Ss should then continue the task on their own as a written exercise. Check Ss' answers around the class.)*

(Suggested answers)

A month ago, I visited my grandmother.
Three years ago, I learnt to ride a bicycle.
Yesterday morning, I went to work.
The day before yesterday, I stayed at home and relaxed.
On my seventh birthday, I had a party.
Last Christmas, I got lots of presents.
Last weekend, I went camping.
Last night, I met some friends.

STUDY TIP (p. 34)

(Present the theory in the Study Tip box preceding the exercise, then help Ss answer the questions in Ex. 11.)

11 In the end, the soldier came back with a huge box of cakes and they all had tea together.
All the people in the story felt happy.

12 a) *(Read aloud the adjectives in the list, and help Ss to match them to the drawings. Check that Ss have clearly grasped the meaning of each word, by using mime/Ss' mother tongue; Ss then say the appropriate word in English, chorally or individually.)*

1	*happy*	5	proud
2	tired	6	confused
3	scared	7	surprised
4	sad	8	angry

b) *(Read each of the sentences aloud and explain/elicit the meaning of any unknown words; Ss say the missing word, chorally or individually.)*

1	happy	5	tired
2	surprised	6	sad
3	angry	7	proud
4	confused	8	scared

WRITING TIP (p. 35)

(Present the theory in the Writing Tip box, and ask Ss to check whether the plan in Ex. 14 conforms to this theory.)

13 a) *(Read aloud the task instructions and explain/ elicit the meaning of **vet**. Ask Ss to look at the pictures, and complete the task orally with the class. Provide Ss with the relevant vocabulary, if necessary [e.g. **knife**].)*

Picture A

1 Jim is at home.
2 It is four o'clock.
3 Jim's pet snake, Slippy.

Picture B

1 They are on the train.
2 Two men are with them.
3 They feel angry.
4 One of the men is holding a knife.
5 They tell Jim to give them his bag.

Picture C

1. They are running away because they saw Slippy.
2. They feel scared.

Picture D

1 They are on the platform.
2 Jim feels proud of Slippy/happy.

b) *(Read aloud each of the items; Ss repeat, chorally or individually, and match the items to the speech bubbles.)*

1 "Give me your bag, now!"
2 "Help! A snake!"

c) *(If desired, ask Ss to give the past tense of each of the verbs used. Then, help individual Ss to narrate the story orally in full sentences; repeat this with various Ss, several times if necessary, to ensure that Ss are thoroughly prepared to cope with Ex. 14.)*

(Suggested answer)

● One afternoon two weeks ago, Jim decided to take his pet snake, Slippy, to the vet. He put Slippy in his sports bag and went to the underground station.

● On the train, Jim noticed two large men. He felt frightened. The two men came up to him. One of the men shouted, "Give me your bag, now!" He had a knife in his hand. The two men looked very angry, so Jim gave them his bag.

● The two men took the bag. They opened it and Slippy's head popped out. One of the men shouted, "Help! A snake!" The two men ran towards the door.

● When the train stopped at the next station, the two men jumped off the train and ran away. Jim was very proud of Slippy.

14 *(Remind Ss to use the title, as well as the beginning and paragraph plan given, then assign the task as written HW.)*

(Ss' own answers. See suggested answer for Ex. 13c.)

Unit 9 - All Creatures Great and Small (pp. 36 - 39)

┌─────────────────────────────────────┐
│ **Objectives** │
└─────────────────────────────────────┘

Vocabulary: animals/pets
Grammar: comparative & superlative forms of adjectives; links of addition/contrast (*also, what is more, however, on the other hand*)
Reading: reading for specific information; reading for detailed understanding
Writing: an article giving the good and bad points about keeping a cat as a pet

1 a) *(Ask Ss to look at the pictures; present the word **pet** and explain/elicit its meaning. If desired, also explain the meaning of the title [i.e. **creatures** means all forms of animal life, including birds/fish/etc; **great** in this context means big, rather than wonderful]. Point to each of the pictures and read aloud the word for each pet; Ss repeat chorally. Then, read questions a) and b) aloud; individual Ss give appropriate personal responses.)*

b) (Suggested answer)

My favourite animal is the hamster.

c) *(Read aloud the list in question c) and explain/elicit the meaning of any unknown vocabulary; also ensure that Ss have grasped the meaning of the superlative form. Individual Ss then offer their opinion. If desired, Ss may ask and answer in open/closed pairs.)*

(Suggested answers)

I think a horse is the most expensive pet/animal to keep.
I think a dog/parrot is the noisiest pet/animal.
I think a cat is the most independent pet/animal.
I think a monkey is the most intelligent pet/animal.
I think a dog is the most loyal pet/animal.
I think a dog/monkey is the most playful pet/animal.
I think a snake is the most dangerous pet/animal.

2 a) *(Read aloud the question and definitions, explaining/eliciting any unknown vocabulary.)*

B (A sentence which starts a paragraph and summarises what the paragraph is about.)

b) *(Ensure that Ss understand the instructions, and explain that the topic sentences have been removed from the article; then, read aloud sentences a to d. Emphasise that Ss do not, at this stage, need to understand every word or read the text for detailed understanding; instead, they should read quickly to grasp the gist of each paragraph. Allow Ss three or four minutes to complete the task, then check Ss' answers.)*

1 b   2 d   3 a   4 c

c) *(Ask the class to identify which paragraph mentions the good points about having a pet dog [Paragraph 2], and which the bad points [Paragraph 3]. Write the headings **Good Points** and **Bad Points** on the board, and ask individual Ss to identify the points mentioned in the text. Write Ss' correct answers under the appropriate headings on the board, and explain/elicit the meaning of any unknown words in the answers.)*

good points: children love them; they obey commands better than most other animals; they never run away

bad points: they need a lot of space; they can cause problems with your neighbours

d) *(Read the questions aloud and explain/elicit the meaning of **state an opinion**. Help Ss to answer the questions appropriately.)*

He believes that dogs make the best pets.
He states his opinion in the last paragraph.

(Explain/Elicit the meaning of any words in the article, including the topic sentences, which Ss still do not understand. Then, individual Ss read the article aloud.)

3 *(Read aloud each of the words in the list. Allow Ss two or three minutes to complete the task, then check Ss' answers by asking individual Ss to read the completed phrases aloud.)*

1 more   3 friend   5 problems
2 obey   4 cause   6 love

4 *(Explain/Elicit the meaning of the words in bold; Ss then complete the task. Check Ss' answers by asking individual Ss to read the corrected sentences aloud.)*

1 quiet   3 cheap   5 clever
2 lazy   4 independent   6 dangerous

5 *(Read aloud the adjectives in Ex.4; Ss identify each as a good point/bad point and complete the table in the S's book accordingly.)*

Good Points	Bad Points
quiet, funny, cheap, loyal, independent, playful, clever, intelligent	*noisy,* lazy, expensive, dangerous

(Individual Ss make appropriate sentences orally; Ss then complete the task as a written exercise.)

(Suggested answers)

- Monkeys are **funny** animals.
  Hamsters are **cheap** to keep.
  Parrots are **noisy** pets.
  Horses are **expensive** to keep.   etc

6 *(Explain/Elicit the meaning of any unknown words, then allow Ss two or three minutes to complete the task. Check Ss' answers by asking individual Ss to read the completed sentences aloud.)*

2 quiet   4 noisy   6 cheap
3 dangerous   5 obedient

STUDY TIP (p. 37)

(Present the use of comparative and superlative forms of adjectives and explain/elicit the meaning of any unknown words.)

25

7 *(Write the headings Adjectives, Comparatives, and Superlatives on the board. Explain/Elicit the meaning of any unknown adjectives. Help Ss to supply the items missing from the table in the S's book, and write these items under the appropriate headings on the board; Ss copy the items into the table in their books.)*

Adjectives	Comparatives	Superlatives
energetic	more energetic	**the most energetic**
cheap	cheaper	the cheapest
dangerous	more dangerous	**the most dangerous**
good	better	**the best**
lazy	lazier	the laziest
bad	**worse**	the worst
expensive	more expensive	**the most expensive**
loyal	**more loyal**	the most loyal
big	**bigger**	the biggest
friendly	friendlier	the friendliest
old	older	**the oldest**
obedient	**more obedient**	the most obedient
safe	safer	**the safest**

*(Erase the words from the board, but do not erase the headings. Under the heading **Adjectives**, list the words **old**, **cheap**, **safe** and **big**. Present and explain the term **syllables**, then point out that the words listed each have one syllable. Ask Ss to spell out the comparative form of each word, and help them to express the rule below, using the Ss' mother tongue if preferred. Repeat this procedure for the superlative form of the words on the board.)*

- The comparative forms of one-syllable adjectives end in **er** (old - old**er**; cheap - cheap**er**). When the adjective ends in **e**, we only add **r** (safe - saf**er**). When the adjective ends in one stressed vowel between two consonants, we double the last consonant and add **er** (big - bigg**er**).

- The superlative forms of one-syllable adjectives end in **est** (old - old**est**). When the adjective ends in **e**, we only add **st** (safe - saf**est**). When the adjective ends in one stressed vowel between two consonants, we double the last consonant and add **est** (big - bigg**est**). The superlative forms of all adjectives are usually preceded by **the**.

*(Under the heading **Adjectives**, write the words **lazy** and **friendly**. Elicit the fact that these words have two syllables, and emphasise that each ends in **y**. Repeat the procedure outlined above.)*

- When an adjective ends in **y**, we form the comparative by dropping the **y** and adding **ier**, and the superlative by dropping the **y** and adding **iest** (lazy - laz**ier** - laz**iest**).

*(As above, write the words **loyal** and **energetic** on the board. Elicit the fact that each has two or more syllables and does not end in **y**. As before, help Ss to express the rule below.)*

- When an adjective has two or more syllables, we usually form the comparative form by placing **more** in front of it. We form the superlative form of such an adjective by placing **the most** in front of it (loyal - **more** loyal - **the most** loyal; energetic - **more** energetic - **the most** energetic).

*(Write the words **good** and **bad** on the board; elicit their comparative and superlative forms, write these on the board, and explain the rule below.)*

- Irregular adjectives have their own individual comparative and superlative forms and do not follow the rules stated above, except in that the superlative forms are usually preceded by **the**.

- We use **in** in the superlative when we talk about places.
  e.g. *He is the tallest **in his class**.*

8 *(Present the examples given in the S's book, emphasising that <u>two groups</u> are being compared, thus requiring the use of comparative form. Explain/Elicit the meaning of **naughty** [5 B]. Allow Ss three or four minutes to complete the task, then check Ss' answers by asking open pairs of Ss to read aloud the short exchanges. Write the comparative forms on the board, reminding Ss of the relevant rule in each case. Finally, Ss read each exchange aloud in closed pairs.)*

2   more energetic, lazier
3   quieter, noisier
4   safer, more dangerous
5   more obedient, naughtier

9 *(Present the example given in the S's book, pointing out that in this exercise <u>all</u> types of pets are compared, thus requiring the use of the superlative forms. Explain/Elicit the meaning of **boring** [5 B]. Repeat the procedure used for Ex. 8.)*

2   laziest   4   strongest
3   nosiest   5   most boring

STUDY TIP (p. 38)

(Present the theory in the Study Tip box, and explain/elicit the meaning of any unknown words. Emphasise that the first list of words is used to join similar points [i.e. two good points, or two bad points] while the second list is used to introduce a contrast [e.g. a bad point following a good point].)

10 *(Ask Ss to scan the text in Ex. 2 in order to find and underline the linking words/phrases. Check Ss' answers, and elicit the fact that the words link similar points within a paragraph, except for **however**, which introduces a list of bad points following the list of good points in the preceding paragraph.)*

a) Also, What is more, Firstly, Secondly
b) However

11 *(Read the first item aloud, and explain/elicit the meaning of **cute** and **dirty**. Elicit the fact that the first sentence presents a good point about rabbits as pets, while the second presents a bad point; therefore **However** is used, to show contrast. Explain/Elicit the meaning of **easy to care for** and **need a lot of space**. Allow Ss about five minutes to complete the task, then check Ss' answers by asking individual Ss to read the corrected sentences aloud.)*

1	However	6	What is more
2	On the other hand	7	Also
3	Also	8	Secondly
4	Firstly	9	On the other hand
5	On the other hand	10	What is more

12 *(Explain/Elicit the meaning of ·**popular, entertaining, amusing, cause** [a problem]**, embarrass, repeat rude words** and **companions** . Allow Ss about five minutes to read the text and fill in the missing words. Check Ss' answers, and remind Ss that the second paragraph lists good points about parrots as pets, while the third paragraph lists bad points.)*

a) 1 Firstly
2 Also/What is more/Secondly
3 Also/What is more
4 On the other hand
5 Also/What is more

(Help Ss to identify the topic sentences, then explain/ elicit the meaning of any words which the Ss still do not understand. Finally, individual Ss read the completed text aloud.)

Topic sentences

Para 1 - Are you looking for a pet?
Para 2 - Parrots are great pets.
Para 3 - On the other hand, parrots can cause problems.
Para 4 - In conclusion, I think that, despite their bad points, parrots make excellent pets.

b) *(Write the heading, shown below, on the board. Help Ss to identify the relevant words/phrases, and complete the table on the board. Ss copy these words/phrases into the tables in their books. Ask individual Ss to make full sentences, orally, using the notes.)*

Good Points	Reasons
• beautiful	• they are brightly coloured
• entertaining and amusing	• they can make you laugh with the things they say
• aren't difficult to look after	• they don't need any exercise

Bad Points	Reasons
• they can embarrass you	• often repeat rude words from the TV or radio
• you can't leave them alone all day	• need to have company

13 *(Read aloud each of the items in the table, and explain/elicit the meaning of any unknown words. Help Ss to match each point to the appropriate reason, then present the introduction to the paragraph. Individual Ss make sentences orally, using the items in the table. Finally, Ss repeat the task as a written exercise.)*

- **Good points** -   2 c   3 a
- **Bad points** -   1 b   2 a

- **(Suggested answer)**

  ... aren't expensive to keep **as** they don't eat a lot. Also, they are easy to look after **because** they don't need much attention.
  ... you can't teach them to do tricks. Also they can bite you, **because** they are frightened of people.

WRITING TIP (p. 39)

(Present the theory in the Writing Tip box and ask Ss to look at the texts in Ex. 2 and Ex. 12 in order to check that they conform to the theory presented here.)

14 *(Ask Ss to read the table of prompts, and explain/elicit the meaning of any unknown words. Explain that these prompts will form the basis of paragraphs 2 and 3 of the article in the Photo File section. Remind Ss that they should use the linking words/expressions given in the Writing Tip box and should follow the plan in the S's book. Help individual Ss to complete the task orally, then assign it as written HW.)*

(Suggested answer)

Cats Can Make the Best Pets

There is no question that a pet can give you pleasure and amusement. There are millions of happy cat owners around the world today who believe that cats make the best pets.

Cats are wonderful pets. Firstly, they make great companions because they are very playful. Secondly, they are easy to look after. They don't need much attention. What is more, they are cheap to keep because their food doesn't cost much.

However, having a cat as a pet has its disadvantages. Firstly, you can't teach them to do tricks as they don't obey commands. Also, they can destroy your furniture because they need to sharpen their claws.

In conclusion, I believe that despite these disadvantages, cats still make the best pets. Why don't you get a cat and find out for yourself?

Unit 10 - Lights! Camera! ACTION! (pp. 40 - 43)

Objectives

Vocabulary: terminology of films/drama; expressing opinion/reactions; recommending
Grammar: adjectives ending in *ing*; the present simple (historic present; links of addition/contrast/reason)
Reading: reading for detailed understanding; scanning for specific information
Writing: a film review

1 a) *(Read aloud the items in the list. Ss repeat, chorally and/or individually. Read questions a to f aloud, and explain/elicit the meaning of any unknown vocabulary. Help Ss to match the listed items to the definitions.)*

a	a comedy	d	a horror film
b	a romance	e	a science-fiction film
c	an action film	f	a cartoon

b) *(Ask Ss to look at the pictures and guess what type of film each is. If necessary, draw Ss' attention to visual clues in the pictures to help them identify the type of film. Then, Ss ask and answer questions in open/closed pairs.)*
e.g. S1: *What type of film is Star Wars?*
S2: *It's a science-fiction film. What type of film is Poltergeist?* etc.

Mad Max 3: an action film
Poltergeist: a horror film
Star Wars: a science-fiction film
Snow White and the Seven Dwarfs: a cartoon
Gone with the Wind: a romance
Home Alone: a comedy

2 *(Explain what a film review is and where one can find such a piece of writing [e.g. newspaper, magazine, etc]. Read questions 1 to 9 aloud and explain/elicit the meaning of any unknown vocabulary. Allow Ss five minutes to read the text, then help individual Ss to answer the questions orally. Explain/Elicit the meaning of any vocabulary in the text which Ss still do not understand, then ask individual Ss to read the text aloud.)*

1 *101 DALMATIANS* is a comedy.
2 Stephen Herek is the director.
3 Glenn Close, Jeff Daniels and Joely Richardson are in the cast.
4 The story takes place in and around London.
5 The main characters are Cruella De Vil, Roger and Anita, their two Dalmatians, Pongo and Perdy, and the adorable puppies.
6 Cruella wants to make a coat from the fur of Dalmatian puppies.
7 Cruella's two assistants steal Pongo and Perdy's puppies.
8 They take them to an old house.
9 Tom thinks *101 DALMATIANS* is an amusing film for the whole family.

3 *(Allow Ss three minutes to do the exercise, then check Ss' answers around the class.)*

2 e	4 i	6 b	8 j	10 f
3 h	5 a	7 c	9 d	

4 *(Read aloud each of the words in the list and explain/elicit their meaning without using the synonyms in bold. Allow Ss about two minutes to complete the task, then check Ss' answers by asking Ss to read aloud each phrase, with the word in bold replaced by its synonym.)*

1 fantastic = great   4 adorable = lovable
2 evil = wicked   5 horrible = awful
3 kind = friendly   6 amusing = funny

5 *(Present the theory in the Study Tip box which precedes the exercise; then present the example in the exercise and explain/elicit the meaning of the verbs in brackets. Allow Ss about three minutes to complete the task, then check Ss' answers. Write the words on the board, pointing out that **boring** and **amazing** drop the final **e** before adding **ing**. Finally, ask individual Ss to read the completed sentences aloud.)*

2 interesting   6 frightening
3 boring   7 amazing
4 thrilling   8 touching
5 disappointing

6 *(Ask individual Ss to make appropriate sentences orally; help them where necessary, with the English titles of films they have seen. Ss should then repeat the task as a written exercise.)*

(Suggested answers)

Sleepless in Seattle is a **touching** film.
Titanic is an **amazing** film.
Scream is a **frightening** film.
Men in Black is an **entertaining** film.
The Postman is a **disappointing** film.

7 *(Read aloud the information about* The Lost World: Jurassic Park *and explain/elicit the meaning of any unknown vocabulary, then complete the paragraph orally with the class. Help individual Ss to talk about the remaining films, using the paragraph for* The Lost World: Jurassic Park *as a model, and explain/elicit the meaning of any unknown vocabulary. As HW, ask Ss to choose one of the three films and write a short paragraph.)*

(Suggested answers)

- ... **Costa Rica**. The main characters are the scientists, **Dr Ian Malcolm** and **Dr Sarah Harding**; the **wicked hunter**, Roland Tembo; and, of course, **the frightening dinosaurs**.

- *Pocahontas* is an amusing cartoon. The story takes place in America. The main characters are the American Indian princess, Pocahontas; Captain John Smith; Chief Powhatan; and John Ratcliffe, the evil Governor.

- *Romeo and Juliet* is a touching romance. The story takes place in Florida. The main characters are Romeo and Juliet, the young couple in love.

- *Murder* is a boring horror film. The story takes place in Austria. The main characters are John Lawless; his friend, Mark; and Phil, John's brother.

8 *(Draw Ss' attention to the final paragraph of the text in Ex. 2, and explain that reviews often end with a **recommendation**; present and explain the term. Read aloud the sentences in the table and explain/elicit the meaning of each; Ss identify whether each is a positive recommendation (♥) or a negative one (✗), and tick the appropriate space in the table.)*

	♥	✗
Don't waste your time watching this film.		✔
Don't miss it!	✔	
It's a must!	✔	
Don't bother with this one.		✔
I definitely recommend it.	✔	

9 **a)** *(Present the example, then ask individual Ss to read aloud each of the remaining sentences, together with an appropriate recommendation. Ss then repeat the task as a written exercise.)*

(Suggested answers)

2 Don't miss it!
3 I definitely recommend it.
4 It's a must!

b) *(Ask Ss to look at their answers in Ex. 6. Ss read these aloud, together with appropriate recommendations, in open/closed pairs. Monitor Ss' performance around the class.)*

(Suggested answers)

- *Men in Black* is an entertaining film. Don't miss it!
- *The Postman* is a disappointing film. Don't bother with this one.

STUDY TIP (p. 42)

(Present the theory in the Study Tip box and explain/elicit the meaning of any unknown vocabulary. Explain that we use the present simple instead of the past simple when we write reviews for films, books and plays. Also, explain the use of and, so and because.)

10 *(Explain that Ss will read the third paragraph of a review of the film Popeye. Ask Ss to say [in their mother tongue, if preferred] what they know about the characters. [Popeye is a sailor, and becomes very strong when he eats spinach; Olive Oyl is tall and thin, loved by both Popeye and Bluto; Bluto is a large, strong villain; etc.] Explain/Elicit the meaning of any unknown vocabulary, and complete the first two items orally with the class. Allow Ss two or three minutes to complete the task. Check Ss' answers, then ask individual Ss to read the completed task aloud.)*

1	because	3	and	5	and
2	and	4	so	6	and

11 *(Ask Ss to look at the picture in Ex. 12 [the character ET and director Steven Spielberg] and say — in their mother tongue, if preferred — what they know about the film. Read the questions aloud and explain/elicit any unknown vocabulary, then explain that these questions have been removed from the dialogue. Complete the first two items orally with the class, emphasising that Ss must read the reply in order to deduce the preceding question. Allow Ss about five minutes to complete the remainder of the task. Check Ss' answers around the class, and explain/elicit the meaning of any vocabulary which Ss still do not understand. Finally, Ss read the dialogue aloud in open/closed pairs.)*

1 Where does the story take place?
2 Who are the main characters?
3 Who is ET?
4 What is the plot of the film?
5 What happens then?
6 How does ET feel?
7 What happens in the end?

WRITING TIP (p. 43)

(Present the theory in the Writing Tip box. Explain/Elicit the meaning of any unknown vocabulary.)

12 *(Ask Ss to look at the plan in the S's book, and prompt them to extract the relevant information from the dialogue in Ex. 11, as shown here.)*

e.g. T: *What is the name of the film?*
S1: *ET The Extra-Terrestrial.*
T: *What type of film is it?*
S2: *It's a science-fiction film.*
T: *Where does the story take place?*
S3: *In a small town in America.*
T: *Who are the main characters?*   etc

Next, help individual Ss to express this information in full sentences, following the model of the text in Ex. 2. Repeat the procedure, if necessary, until satisfied that Ss can complete the task orally. Assign the task as written HW, reminding Ss to use the picture in the Photo File section.)

(Suggested answer)

ET The Extra-Terrestrial, is a touching science-fiction film.

The story takes place in a small town in America. The main characters are Elliott, a young boy; Mike and Gertie, his brother and sister; and, of course, ET.

ET is a lovable creature from outer space. Elliott finds ET when the other aliens leave Earth without him. Elliott takes ET to his house to hide him, and, together with his brother and sister, he takes care of him. They also teach him things about life on Earth. ET loves his new friends, but he misses his family and wants to return home. The children find a way to help him return home and their adventure begins.

ET The Extra-Terrestrial is a great film! I definitely recommend it.

Unit 11 - Take my Advice (pp. 44 - 47)

1 passport	3 under	5 forget
2 one	4 German marks	

```
┌─────────────────┐
│    Objectives   │
└─────────────────┘
```

Vocabulary: travel preparations; home safety
Grammar: the imperative; *must/mustn't;*
should/shouldn't; clauses of purpose/reason
Reading: skimming; scanning; reading for
specific information
Writing: a friendly letter of advice

1 *(Present the terms* **take [sb's] advice/give [sb] advice** *and* **travel abroad,** *and explain/elicit their meaning. If desired, ask Ss to suggest, in their mother tongue, some problems one might face when travelling abroad and how these might be avoided.)*

a) *(Ask Ss to look at the pictures. Read the items in the list aloud; Ss repeat, chorally or individually. Help Ss match the items to the pictures, and check that they have fully understood the meaning of the items.)*

1 C   2 A   3 B   4 D

b) *(Explain the imaginary situation, ensuring Ss know that Frankfurt is in Germany. Emphasise that the trip is planned for the future and the advice is given in order to avoid potential problems rather than solve existing ones. Explain that* **must** *and* **should** *are used to give advice; it is not necessary, at this stage, to present further details of their use. Explain/Elicit the meaning of any other unknown vocabulary in the sentences, and help Ss to fill in the missing words correctly. Check that Ss have fully understood the advice, and ask individual Ss to read the completed sentences aloud.)*

1 airport	3 German marks
2 passport	4 luggage

2 *(Explain that Karen is going — i.e. in the future — to Frankfurt on holiday, and has written to her friend, Claire, to tell her the news; the letter which Ss will read is Claire's reply, giving Karen advice. Read aloud the sentences which follow the text, and explain/elicit the meaning of any unknown vocabulary. Emphasise that Ss do not need to read for detailed understanding at this stage, but should "skim" the text to find the relevant sections. Allow Ss two or three minutes to complete the task, then check Ss' answers.)*

(Ask questions to elicit the reason given in support of each piece of advice, and explain/elicit the meaning of any unknown vocabulary. Finally, individual Ss read the text of the letter aloud.)

3 *(Allow Ss two or three minutes to complete the task. Check Ss' answers, then read aloud each of the words in the list; Ss respond, chorally or individually, by saying the relevant completed phrase.)*

1 great	4 check	7 heavy
2 travel	5 companies	8 trip
3 useful	6 charge	

STUDY TIP (p. 45)

(Present the use of **should/shouldn't** *and* **must/mustn't,** *and explain/elicit the meaning of any unknown vocabulary in the Study Tip box. Ensure that Ss grasp the distinction of "strong" advice [i.e. where failure to follow the advice would have serious consequences].)*

4 *(Ask Ss to scan the letter in Ex. 2 again in order to find and underline the advice introduced by* **should** *and* **must.** *Elicit that* **should** *= "a good idea" and* **must** *= necessary.)*

GOOD IDEA - keep luggage under twenty kilos
           - change pounds into German marks
NECESSARY - take passport
           - arrive at the airport at least one
             hour before the flight leaves

(Help Ss to explain [in their mother tongue, if necessary] the consequences of ignoring each piece of advice; point out that not having German marks on arrival/paying extra for excess luggage is inconvenient, but missing one's flight/being unable to leave the country is a major problem which would make it impossible to go on holiday at all.)

5 *(Ask Ss to look at the picture and identify the various objects shown. Ensure that Ss understand the situation, then read aloud the advice and reasons in the table, and explain/elicit any unknown words. Ss match each tip to the relevant reason, then individual Ss make appropriate sentences orally.)*

2 d   3 a   4 c

You **should** bring your camera **to** take pictures of the sights.
You **should** buy a map **to** make sure you don't get lost.
You **should** pack some jumpers **to** keep you warm.

6 *(Present the situation, pointing out that Bob is travelling by plane. Check that Ss understand* **smoke**, **mobile phones**, **plane ticket**, **carry diseases**, **cigarettes** *and* **cause fires**; *explain/elicit the meaning of any unknown items. Ss match the advice and reasons. Check Ss' answers, and point out that the reasons listed imply serious consequences, so the advice given is "strong" advice, expressed using* **must/mustn't**. *Individual Ss make appropriate sentences orally.)*

2 d   3 a   4 c

You **mustn't** smoke on the plane **because** cigarettes can cause fires.
You **mustn't** use mobile phones on the plane **because** they can affect planes' computers.
You **must** take your plane ticket **because** you can't get on the plane without it.

STUDY TIP (p. 45)

(Present the use of imperatives for written warnings and explain/elicit the use of any unknown vocabulary. Explain that although the imperative is appropriate for signs/notices, its use in other circumstances might seem impolite; instead, we use **must/ mustn't**.*)*

7 *(Read aloud each of the items in the list, explaining/ eliciting the meaning of any unknown words, and help Ss to match each description to the relevant sign. Ask individual Ss to explain the first two or three signs using* **must/mustn't**; *Ss then complete the task as a written exercise. Check Ss' answers by asking individual Ss to read their sentences aloud.)*

2 d - You **must** stop here.
3 g - You **mustn't** park here.
4 e - You **mustn't** litter.
5 b - You **must** drive slowly.
6 h - You **mustn't** enter here.
7 a - You **mustn't** swim here.
8 f - You **mustn't** turn right.

8 *(Explain that each of the pictures shows a potential danger threatening the safety of children in the home. Read aloud each of the items in the list, explaining/eliciting the meaning of any unknown words, and ask the class to match the items to the pictures. Point out that since the danger is so great in each situation, the advice given to parents will be expressed using* **must/mustn't**. *Complete the first two or three sentences orally with the class; Ss then complete the task as a written exercise. Check Ss' answers by asking individual Ss to read their sentences aloud.)*

2 c   3 f   4 d   5 a   6 e

9 **a)** *(Ensure that Ss understand the situation, and explain/elicit the meaning of any unknown words in the instructions. Ask Ss to read the letter quickly in order to find and underline the phrases giving advice. Check Ss' answers, and elicit the fact the strong advice is in Paragraph 2.)*

(Phrases to be underlined:)
Para 2 - you must bring a tent and sleeping bag
 - you must always put it [i.e. your camp fire] out before you go to sleep
 - you mustn't play loud music
 - you mustn't leave any rubbish behind
Para 3 - you should bring a torch
 - [you should bring] insect repellent
 - you shouldn't forget to pack a jumper

(Explain/Elicit the meaning of any unknown vocabulary in the text; individual Ss then read the text aloud.)

b) *(On the board, write the table as it appears in the S's book. Ask Ss to look at the letter again and find the missing phrases; use Ss' answers to complete the table on the board.)*

Must/Mustn't	Reasons
• bring a tent and sleeping bag	• **Grizedale National Park does not provide them**
• **put out camp fire before going to sleep**	• avoid forest fires
• not play loud music	• **the noise disturbs the other campers**
• **leave any rubbish behind**	• it harms the environment
Should/Shouldn't	**Reasons**
• **bring a torch**	• help you see in the dark
• bring insect repellent	• **protect yourself from mosquitoes**
• **not forget to pack a jumper**	• keep you warm on chilly evenings

*(Ask Ss to check whether the text uses to or **because** in each piece of advice, then ask Ss to close their books. Individual Ss make appropriate sentences orally.)*

You **must** bring a tent and sleeping bag **because** Grizedale National Park does not provide them.
You **must** put out camp fires before going to sleep **to** avoid forest fires.
You **mustn't** play loud music **because** the noise disturbs the other campers.
You **mustn't** leave any rubbish behind **because** it harms the environment.
You **should** bring a torch **to** help you see in the dark.
You **should** bring insect repellent **to** protect yourself from mosquitoes.
You **shouldn't** forget to pack a jumper **to** keep you warm on chilly evenings.

10 *(Present the examples given in the S's book, and explain/elicit the meaning of any unknown vocabulary in the exercise. Allow Ss three or four minutes to complete the task, then check Ss' answers by asking individual Ss to read their sentences aloud.)*

3   You shouldn't drink alcohol.
4   You mustn't eat fatty foods before you fly.
5   You should use traveller's cheques.
6   You mustn't wear expensive jewellery.
7   You should book a hotel before you leave.
8   You must drink bottled water.

11 *(Ensure that Ss understand the situation, then read the phrases in the table aloud and explain/elicit the meaning of any unknown vocabulary. Ss match the advice to the relevant reasons. Check Ss' answers, and help individual Ss to make appropriate sentences orally.)*

1 c   3 d   5 f   7 e
2 a   4 b   6 g

1   You must buy a road map **to** help you find your way.
2   You must take a first aid kit with you **because** there is always a danger of accidents.
3   You must check the car engine **to** make sure it is in good condition.
4   You mustn't exceed the speed limit **because** you can cause an accident.
5   You should drive on the main roads **to** avoid getting lost.
6   You should listen to the weather forecast **to** find out what clothes you need to take.
7   You shouldn't travel alone **because** it is dangerous.

WRITING TIP (p. 47)

(Present the theory in the Writing Tip box and explain/elicit the meaning of any unknown vocabulary.)

12 *(Ensure that Ss understand the situation and instructions. Read aloud the plan in the S's book and explain/elicit the meaning of any unknown vocabulary. Elicit the fact that Ss will use the advice from the **must/mustn't** column of Ex. 11 for Paragraph 2, and from the **should/shouldn't** column for Paragraph 3. Help individual Ss to complete the task orally using **first of all, also** etc as in the letter in Ex. 2. Finally, assign the task as written HW.)*

(Suggested answer)

40 Redhill Road
Sydney 2001
New South Wales
Australia
24th May, ...

Dear James,
  Great to hear from you again! I went on a similar trip around Europe five years ago — it was great! Here are some tips to help you with your trip.
  First of all, you must buy a road map to help you find your way. You must take a first aid kit with

33

you because there is always a danger of accidents. Also, you must check the car engine to make sure it is in good condition. Finally, you mustn't exceed the speed limit because you can cause an accident.

Of course, you should drive on the main roads to avoid getting lost. Also, you should listen to the weather forecast to find out what clothes you need to take. Remember, you shouldn't travel alone, because it is dangerous.

Keep these tips in mind and you shouldn't have any problems. Hope to hear from you soon.

Yours,
Bill

Unit 12 - A Red Rag to a Bull! (pp. 48 - 51)

Objectives

Vocabulary: adjectives/adverbs related to stories
Grammar: the past simple; similes; the conjunctions *and, but, so;* adjectives; adverbs
Reading: reading for detailed understanding; scanning
Writing: a story

1 a) *(Explain to Ss the meaning of the title, and mention that bulls are widely [though wrongly] believed to react aggressively to the colour red. Ask Ss to look at the pictures, and draw their attention to the numbered circles. Read the items in the list aloud and explain/elicit the meaning of any unknown vocabulary. Ss match the items to the numbers and fill in the boxes accordingly.)*

1	Bernie the bull	5	trousers
2	Jeff Monk	6	gate
3	horns	7	Jeff's wife
4	bucket		

b) *(Read the sentences aloud. Ss match them to the pictures. Check Ss' answers, and explain/elicit the meaning of any unknown vocabulary.)*

1 D	2 B	3 A	4 C

2 *(Read the verbs in the list aloud, and explain/elicit the meaning of any unknown vocabulary. Elicit the past form of the verbs, reminding Ss that they may consult the list of irregular verbs on p. 64 if necessary.)*

laughed, had, said, ran, shouted, put ... on, called, dropped, lived, bought

(Complete the first two or three examples orally with the class. Allow Ss about five minutes to complete the remainder of the task. Check Ss' answers, then ask individual Ss in turn to read the text aloud. Explain/Elicit the meaning of any unknown vocabulary.)

1	lived	5	put ... on	9	ran
2	had	6	called	10	laughed
3	said	7	dropped		
4	bought	8	shouted		

3 *(Present the example given in the S's book, and complete the first question or two orally with the class. Allow Ss four or five minutes to complete the remainder of the task, monitoring Ss' performance while they work. Finally, ask individual Ss to read the completed questions aloud.)*

1 ... was Jeff's favourite animal
2 ... old was Bernie
3 ... did Jeff's wife buy him
4 ... did Jeff go to the field
5 ... began to run angrily towards Jeff
6 ... did Jeff do
7 ... did Jeff shout loudly to his wife
8 ... did Jeff run to
9 ... did Bernie do
10 ... did Jeff's wife do ...

4 *(Present the example given in the S's book, then allow Ss three or four minutes to find the correct facts. Check Ss' answers by asking individual Ss to correct the mistakes orally.)*

2 He didn't have a few animals. He had **a lot of** animals.
3 His favourite wasn't a horse called Bernie. His favourite/It was **a bull** called Bernie.
4 His wife didn't buy him a cheap blue shirt. She/His wife bought him **an expensive red** shirt.
5 Bernie didn't (look up and) give a quiet snort. He/Bernie (looked up and) gave a **loud** snort.
6 He didn't run happily towards Jeff. He ran **angrily** towards Jeff.
7 His wife didn't shout when she saw him without his trousers. She/His wife **laughed** when she saw him without his trousers.

34

5 *(Explain that Ss must rearrange the letters in bold to form the word defined and check that Ss understand the vocabulary in the definitions. Ss complete the task, in pairs or small groups, if desired. Check Ss' answers and write the correct words on the board.)*

1	dangerous	3	snort
2	feed	4	favourite

6 *(Allow Ss two or three minutes to complete the task, then check Ss' answers by asking individual Ss to read the corrected sentences aloud.)*

1	on	3	up	5	towards	7	into
2	on	4	over	6	to	8	off

STUDY TIP (p. 49)

(Present the theory in the Study Tip box, then ask Ss to scan the text in Ex. 2 in order to find and underline the adjectives used.)

red (rag), quiet (farm), careful (Jeff), dangerous (bulls), expensive red (shirt), loud (snort), long (horns), new (shirt)

7 *(Read the adjectives in the list aloud, and explain/ elicit their meaning without using the synonyms in bold from the exercise which follows. Allow Ss two or three minutes to complete the task, then check Ss' answers. Ask individual Ss to read the sentences aloud, with the adjectives from the list in place of the synonyms in bold.)*

2	pretty	4	scary	6	cheerful
3	huge	5	horrible		

STUDY TIP (p. 49)

(Present the theory in the Study Tip box, then ask Ss to scan the text in Ex. 2 in order to find and underline the adverbs used.)

suddenly (gave ...), (run) angrily, (ran ...) fast, (shouted) loudly, Fortunately (...came off), (ran) quickly

8 *(Allow Ss two or three minutes to complete the task, then check Ss' answers by asking individual Ss to read the completed sentences aloud.)*

1	cheerfully	3	slowly	5	badly
2	quickly	4	loudly	6	carefully

9 *(Read the adverbs in the list aloud and explain/elicit their meaning. Complete the first item or two orally*

with the class, then allow Ss about three minutes to complete the remainder of the task on their own. Check Ss' answers, and ask individual Ss to read the completed text aloud.)*

1	carefully	3	quickly	5	well
2	loudly	4	beautifully	6	wickedly

STUDY TIP (p. 50)

(Present the theory in the Study Tip box and explain/ elicit the meaning of any unknown vocabulary. Point out that the use of direct speech makes the story more dramatic, therefore more interesting to the reader. Also, point out that inverted commas are absolutely necessary when we write someone's exact words.)

10 *(Ask individual Ss to read the speech bubbles aloud. Elicit examples of situations in which these words might be used.*
    e.g. "Time to get up!" : a parent to his/her child
        "Please be quiet!" : a teacher to his/her Ss
        "Help!" : someone who is in danger (e.g. his/her house is on fire)
        "Good evening, madam. Can I help you?" : a shop assistant to a customer
Read sentences 1 to 4 and explain/elicit the meaning of any unknown vocabulary. Allow Ss two or three minutes to fill in the gaps with the appropriate words. Check Ss' answers by asking individual Ss to read the completed sentences aloud.)

1 Help!
2 Time to get up!
3 Please be quiet!
4 Good evening, madam. Can I help you?

STUDY TIP (p. 50)

(Present the theory in the Study Tip box and explain/ elicit the meaning of any unknown words.)

11 *(Ask Ss to look at the table, and help them to match the verbs to the nouns to make similes. Explain the similes. Allow Ss three or four minutes to fill the gaps in the sentences. Check Ss' answers by asking individual Ss to read the completed sentences aloud.)*

2	d	3 e	4 f	5 b	6 a				

1	like an angel	4	like a king
2	like a fish	5	like the wind
3	like a ballerina	6	like a mother

12 *(Read the examples aloud, eliciting from Ss the use of **and, so** and **but** [i.e. **and** is used to link similar/ non-contrasting ideas, **so** is used to express result, **but** is used to link opposing ideas]. Explain/Elicit the meaning of these words/phrases: **start the car, smoke, engine, fire extinguisher, locked, thief, bit, leg, alright, in the end**. Complete the first two items orally with the class, then allow Ss about five minutes to complete the remainder of the task. Check Ss' answers by asking individual Ss to read the compound sentences aloud.)*

1   It was a warm sunny day, **so** we decided to go on a picnic.
2   We got our things ready **and** put them in the car.
3   Simon tried to start the car, **but** smoke began to come out of the engine.
4   We jumped out quickly **and** ran to get a fire extinguisher.
5   The door was locked, **so** we couldn't get into the house.
6   One of the windows was open, **so** Simon climbed into the house.
7   Our dog thought Simon was a thief, **so** he bit his leg.
8   Simon was alright in the end, **but** we didn't go on a picnic that day!

13 *(Read the first sentence aloud and present the mistake and its correction. Tell Ss that there are eight further mistakes [of grammar, spelling or punctuation]. Allow Ss five minutes to read the remainder of the story and underline the words they think are wrong. Ask individual Ss to read portions of the story aloud and correct the mistakes. Write the correct words on the board.)*

a) walked   (line 6)   -   walk
        heared   (line 7)   -   heard
        babys   (line 9)   -   baby's
        thinked (line 12) -   thought
        run   (line 14) -   ran
        has   (line 16) -   have
        freinds (line 20) -   friends
        lucky   (line 21) -   Lucky

b) *(Allow Ss about five or six minutes to complete the task, then check Ss' answers.)*

- **Adjectives:**
  deep (snow), strange (sound), huge white (dog), hungry (dog), red (shape), young (woman), warm (hospital bed), glad (Sally), new (friends), brave (dog)

- **Adverbs:**
  suddenly (heard), (ran) quickly, (looked) closely, (said) quietly

14 *(Explain that the dialogue is from an interview between Josh Bell [J], and a magazine reporter [R] who will write the story of Josh's experience to be printed in the magazine. Remind Ss that they may consult the list of irregular verbs on p. 64, and allow them about five minutes to put the verbs in the past simple. Check Ss' answers around the class, and write these answers on the board. Explain/Elicit the meaning of any unknown vocabulary in the dialogue. Ask Ss to read the completed dialogue aloud in open pairs.)*

1 worked	5 panicked	9 came
2 felt	6 told	10 held
3 was	7 began	11 had
4 saw	8 sped	

15 *(Ask Ss to look at the pictures in the Photo File section and read the beginning given. Then, elicit appropriate answers from Ss to the questions listed in the paragraph plan. Help individual Ss to tell the story orally, then assign the task as written HW. Point out that Ss should use the words in the speech bubbles in their stories.)*

(Suggested answers to the questions in the plan.)
Paragraph 1
- The story happened last summer.
- Josh worked as a lifeguard on a popular beach.
- He felt a little anxious.
- It was a hot sunny day.

Paragraphs 2 - 3
- He saw a large grey shape in the sea.
- He panicked and told everyone to get out of the water.
- They began to swim quickly to the shore.
- The lifeboat crew sped out immediately because they wanted to check that everything was alright.
- They came back five minutes later.
- He held something up for Josh to see.
- He had a grey surfboard.

(Suggested answer)

    ... Suddenly, Josh saw a large grey shape in the sea. Josh panicked and shouted through the megaphone, "Get out of the water!" Then, everyone began to swim quickly to the shore.

The lifeboat crew sped out immediately to check that everything was alright. Josh waited nervously for them to return. Five minutes later, they came back. One of the crew held something up for Josh to see. He had a grey surfboard in his hands. "Don't worry!" the man laughed cheerfully. "This one hasn't got teeth!"

Josh felt silly but at least no one was hurt.

Unit 13 - Going North (pp. 52 - 55)

Objectives

Vocabulary: holidays; tourist attractions; activities; sightseeing
Grammar: be going to; present continuous (future meaning); to-infinitive (infinitive of purpose)
Reading: reading for specific information; scanning
Writing: a letter to a friend about your holiday plans

1 *(Ask Ss to look at the pictures and guess where the young woman is planning to go [Copenhagen]. Read aloud the names of the places in the pictures, then read aloud the phrases in the two columns and explain/elicit the meaning of any unknown vocabulary. Check that Ss can match the phrases to the pictures correctly.)*

an antiques market	-	4
people on a boat trip	-	5
a statue of a mermaid	-	2
a guard	-	1
a canal	-	5
a palace	-	1
a brewery	-	6

2 *(Explain that Melanie, the young woman in the picture, is planning to go on holiday to Copenhagen, and has written to her friend about her future plans. Read the questions aloud, and point out that the answer to the fourth question involves several activities. Allow Ss about five minutes to read the letter and prepare their answers. Help individual Ss to answer the questions orally, and remind Ss that these plans refer to the future. Explain/Elicit the meaning of any unknown vocabulary in the text, then ask individual Ss to read portions of the letter aloud.)*

1 Melanie is going to Copenhagen.
2 She is going to stay there for two weeks.
3 She is going on holiday on 2nd June.
4 She is going to see the Little Mermaid and the changing of the guard at Amalienborg Palace. She's also going to visit Tivoli, and go on a boat trip on the Nyhavn Canal. She is going to visit the antiques market on Gammel Strand and the Carlsberg Brewery, too.
5 She is really excited.

3 *(Allow Ss about three minutes to complete the task. Check Ss' answers by reading aloud each of the words in the list; Ss respond, chorally and/or individually, by reading aloud the completed phrase to which the word belongs.)*

1	holiday	4	guard
2	amusement	5	boat
3	buy	6	antiques

4 *(Repeat the procedure suggested for Ex. 3; then, help individual Ss to make appropriate sentences orally. If desired, Ss may then repeat the latter part of the task as a written exercise.)*

1	great	3	famous
2	wonderful	4	beautiful

(Suggested answers)

1 John's got some **great** news — he's going to be in Paris for a week.
2 I am going to the **wonderful** city of Copenhagen in July.
3 Tivoli is a very **famous** amusement park.
4 There are some **beautiful** statues in the museum.

STUDY TIP (p. 53)

*(Present the theory in the Study Tip box and explain/elicit the meaning of **plans/intentions** and **fixed arrangements**. Point out that in the first picture montage, the speaker has not yet got his passport or bought a ticket — i.e. no definite arrangements [dates, times, etc] have been made; in the second, the speaker has made these arrangements. Explain that when we talk about our plans or things we intend to do, we use 'be going to'. However, we use the present continuous to talk about fixed arrangements.)*

5 *(Ensure that Ss understand the situation and explain that Helen has bought her plane ticket with a fixed return date, and has booked a hotel room. These are therefore arrangements, whereas her sightseeing activities will be arranged after her arrival in London.*

Ask individual Ss to make appropriate sentences orally; if desired, Ss then repeat the task as a written exercise.)

Helen is going to visit Trafalgar Square.
Helen is staying at the Savoy Hotel.
Helen is going to see Big Ben.
Helen is going to rent a car.
Helen is going to visit the British Museum.
Helen is coming back on 2nd July.

STUDY TIP (p. 53)

(Present the theory in the Study Tip box and explain/ elicit the meaning of any unknown words.)

6 *(Copy the table in the S's book onto the board. Ask Ss to scan the text in Ex. 2 and find the phrases missing from the table. Use Ss' answers to complete the table on the board, then ask individual Ss to make appropriate sentences orally.)*

- She is going to visit Tivoli to go on the rides.
- She is going to visit the antiques market to buy some souvenirs.
- She is going to visit the Carlsberg Brewery to see how they make beer.

7 *(Explain/Elicit the meaning of any unknown vocabulary. Help Ss to match the plans to the reasons. Present the sentence given as an example in the S's book, drawing Ss' attention to the words **going to visit**. Explain that when the main verb is **go**, as in the third item, the **going to** form would be clumsy [**going to go to**] and is not used. Instead, we use present continuous − "I am **going to** the antiques market ..." Ask individual Ss to make complete sentences orally.)*

2 c I am going to find a nice restaurant to have lunch.
3 d I am going to the antiques market to buy some souvenirs.
4 b I am going to visit the Royal Theatre to see a play.
5 a I am going on a boat trip to enjoy the interesting sights.

8 *(Ensure that Ss understand the situation, and explain that the references in the "thought bubbles" are to tourist attractions in Prague [capital of the Czech Republic]. Read aloud the adjectives in the list and explain/elicit their meaning. Complete the first two "thought bubbles" orally with the class, then allow Ss two or three minutes to complete the remainder of the task. Check Ss' answers, and explain/elicit the*

meaning of any vocabulary which Ss still don't understand. Finally, ask individual Ss to read the completed sentences aloud.)

2 historic   5 fascinating
3 famous   6 delicious
4 relaxing

(Reasons)

1 ... to enjoy the lovely view.
2 ... to take some pictures.
3 ... to admire the famous paintings and statues.
4 ... to see more of Prague.
5 ... to see the fascinating medieval clock.
6 ... to have a cup of coffee and some delicious pancakes.

9 **a)** *(Ensure that Ss understand the situation and instructions. Read the notes aloud and explain/ elicit the meaning of any unknown vocabulary; if necessary, explain that the references are to famous tourist attractions in Rome. Remind Ss that in the third note we do not use "**going to go to** [see Ex. 7]. Complete the first sentence orally with the class, then allow Ss four or five minutes to complete the remainder of the task. Check Ss' answers, and ask individual Ss to read the completed letter aloud.)*

(Suggested answer)

- I am flying there on Wednesday 20th September, in the afternoon.
- **First,** I am going to visit the Colosseum and the Roman Forum to admire the ancient temples and monuments.
- **Then,** I am going to the famous Fontana di Trevi to throw a coin in and make a wish.
- I am **also** going to visit the Piazza di Spagna to see the artists.
- **Finally,** I am going to walk along the famous Via Veneto to do some window shopping.

b) *(Read each of the questions aloud and help individual Ss to provide appropriate answers orally.)*

1 Jane's address is at the top of the letter.
2 Jane begins her letter with "Dear Mark".
3 In the first paragraph, Jane mentions where she is going (*Rome*) and how long she is planning to stay there (*a week*).
4 The second paragraph is about when she is flying to Rome and the things she is going to see and do there.

5 The third paragraph is about how she feels about her trip (*thrilled*).

6 Jane ends her letter with "Love, Jane".

WRITING TIP (p. 55)

(Present the theory in the Writing Tip box. Ensure that Ss remember the distinction between fixed arrangements and plans/intentions, and remind them that we avoid the use of "be going to go".)

10 **a)** *(Explain that the pictures show famous tourist attractions in Paris. Read each of the prompts aloud and explain/elicit the meaning of any unknown vocabulary. Complete the first item orally with the class; Ss then complete the remainder of the task in closed pairs. Monitor Ss' performance around the class, then check Ss' answers by asking individual Ss to read the completed sentences aloud.)*

1 I am going to the Eiffel Tower to enjoy the spectacular view of the city.

2 I am going to visit the famous Notre Dame Cathedral to take pictures.

3 I am going to spend a day at the Louvre to look at the wonderful paintings and statues.

4 I am going on a boat trip on the Seine to see more of Paris.

5 I am going to the Left Bank to have a cup of coffee and a croissant.

6 I am going to book a table at Maxim's to taste some delicious French dishes.

7 I am going to visit Versailles to walk around the palace and its beautiful gardens.

b) *(Ask Ss to read the plan, then ask questions to elicit information.*
    e.g.   T: Where are you going?
       S1: To Paris.
       T: How long are you staying there?
       S2: Two weeks.   etc
Help individual Ss to complete the task orally, following the model of the letter in Ex. 2. When satisfied that Ss can cope with the task adequately, assign it as written HW.)

(Suggested answer)

13 Cooper Street
London
NW6 IJT

14th July, ...

Dear Lynne,
    I've got some exciting news. I'm going on holiday to Paris for two weeks.
    I'm flying there on Tuesday 21st July, in the morning. First, I am going to the Eiffel Tower to enjoy the spectacular view of the city. Then, I am going to spend a day at the Louvre to look at the wonderful paintings and statues. I am also going to visit the famous Notre Dame Cathedral to take pictures. I am also going to the Left Bank to have a cup of coffee and a croissant. Finally, I'm going to visit Versailles to walk around the palace and its beautiful gardens.
    I am really excited because I know it is going to be a fantastic holiday. Bye for now.

Love,
Lisa

Unit 14 - Getting Ready (pp. 56 - 59)

Objectives
Vocabulary: words related to special occasions/celebrations **Grammar:** the present perfect, **yet**, **already**, **just** **Reading:** reading for specific information; reading for gist **Writing:** a letter to a friend about your birthday party

*(Explain/Elicit the meaning of **to get ready [for sth]**, used in the title, and present the synonym **make preparations**. Explain that the pictures are related to preparations for a typical English wedding.[Ensure that Ss understand the word **wedding** correctly, especially those features of a wedding celebration which may not be customary in the Ss' country/culture.])*

1 *(Read aloud each of the items in the list; Ss repeat, chorally and/or individually. Explain/Elicit the meaning of each item; Ss match the items to the pictures, and number the boxes accordingly.)*

a	5	c	6	e	8	g	4
b	1	d	2	f	7	h	3

2 *(Explain that Cindy is getting married soon, and has written to her friend, Jane, about the wedding preparations. Read aloud the statements which follow the letter, and explain/elicit the meaning of any unknown vocabulary. [If necessary, briefly explain the use of the present perfect:*

e.g. → She has chosen her wedding dress. She chose it last week.

She hasn't ordered the flowers. She's going to order them tomorrow.]

Allow Ss five or six minutes to read the letter silently and mark the statements as true or false. Check Ss' answers around the class. Explain/Elicit the meaning of any vocabulary in the letter which Ss still do not understand then ask individual Ss to read the letter aloud.)

1 F	3 F	5 T	7 T
2 T	4 F	6 F	8 F

3 *(Allow Ss about three minutes to complete the task. Then, read aloud each of the words in the list; Ss respond, chorally or individually, by saying the relevant completed phrase.)*

1 chance	3 busy	5 book	7 all
2 ages	4 care	6 time	

STUDY TIP (p. 57)

(Present the theory in the Study Tip box and explain any unfamiliar grammatical terms. Refer Ss to p. 64 to see the past participles of various irregular verbs.)

4 *(Help Ss to find and underline the present perfect forms.)*

Present Perfect Forms:
Para. 1 - have been, haven't had
Para. 2 - have chosen, have ordered, have decided, have ... replied, have helped, has ... booked, has taken care of
Para. 3 - haven't done, haven't decided, haven't hired, haven't found

*(Write the headings **Regular** and **Irregular** on the board. Ask Ss to identify each underlined verb as regular or irregular; write each past participle on the board under the appropriate heading. Ask Ss to look at p.64 and find the parts of the irregular verbs on the board.)*

Regular:
ordered, decided, replied, helped, booked, hired

Irregular:
been, had, chosen, taken, done, found

5 *(Allow Ss five or six minutes to complete the task. Check Ss' answers around the class.)*

1 written	7 bought	13 given
2 been	8 seen	14 gone
3 told	9 come	15 left
4 sent	10 drunk	16 made
5 thought	11 eaten	17 taken
6 boiled	12 packed	18 organised

STUDY TIP (p. 57)

(Explain the use of the present perfect, and present the time expressions used with this tense. Write these sentences on the board and explain how each time expression is used. Also point out the position of each expression within the sentence structure.
*I haven't seen her **since** Monday. [since: point in time]*
*I haven't seen her **for** three days. [for: duration]*
*Have you **ever** been abroad? [ever: in questions]*
*I have **never** been abroad.*
[have never = I haven't: negative sentences]
*I haven't seen her **yet**. [yet: in negative sentences]*
*Have you seen her **yet**? [yet: in questions]*
*I have **already** talked to her. [already: in the affirmative]*
*I have **just** talked to her. [just: in the affirmative]*
*I have typed three letters **so far**. [so far: in the affirmative])*

6 *(Ensure that Ss understand the situation, then read aloud the prompts in the list and explain/elicit the meaning of any unknown vocabulary. Present the examples given in the S's book, drawing Ss' attention to the position of **already**/**yet** in the sentence. Allow Ss three or four minutes to complete the task; check Ss' answers by asking individual Ss to read the sentences aloud.)*

- Peter **has already boiled** some eggs.
- Peter **hasn't made** a salad **yet**.
- Peter **hasn't packed** the picnic basket **yet**.
- Peter **hasn't put** a blanket in the car **yet**.
- Peter **has already checked** the weather forecast.

7 *(Explain/Elicit the meaning of any unknown vocabulary in the exercise, then complete the first short exchange orally with the class. Allow Ss about three minutes to complete the remainder of the task. Check Ss' answers around the class; then read the short exchanges aloud in open/closed pairs).*

1 A: Have you packed   3 A: has he done
   B: haven't had   B: has hired
2 A: Have you ordered   4 A: Has she sent
   B: have decided   B: has been

8 *(Complete the first two examples orally with the class, and explain/elicit the meaning of any unknown vocabulary in the exercise. Allow Ss two or three minutes to complete the remainder of the task, and check Ss' answers by asking individual Ss to read the corrected sentences aloud.)*

1	already	4	just	7	yet
2	since	5	ever	8	so far
3	never	6	for		

9 *(Present the situation and explain/elicit the meaning of any unknown vocabulary in the prompts. Present the example given in the S's book, and help individual Ss to complete the remainder of the task orally. Ss then repeat the task as a written exercise.)*

They haven't booked a removal van yet.
They have already told their friends their new address.
They haven't cleaned their new house yet.
They have already bought some new furniture.
They haven't walked around their new neighbourhood yet
They have already bought some new curtains.

WRITING TIP (p. 58)

(Present the theory in the Writing Tip box and explain/elicit the meaning of any unknown vocabulary.)

10 **a)** *(Explain that the letter, concerning preparations for a school performance of a musical, is shown here with the paragraphs in the wrong order. Emphasise that Ss do not, at this stage, need to read for detailed understanding; they should read each paragraph quickly to understand the gist, then decide on the correct order of the paragraphs, with the help of the theory in the Writing Tip box if necessary. Allow Ss four or five minutes to complete the task, then check Ss' answers. Explain/Elicit the meaning of any unknown vocabulary, then ask individual Ss to read the letter aloud, with the paragraphs in the correct order.)*

A 3   B 1   C   4   D 2

b) *(Complete the task orally with the class, then ask Ss to check that the paragraph plan of Emily's letter conforms to the theory in the Writing Tip box.)*

a) third   b) fourth   c) first   d) second

11 *(Ensure that Ss understand the situation and instructions, then read the prompts aloud and explain/elicit the meaning of any unknown vocabulary. Explain that Ss will use the prompts to make sentences as in Ex. 6. Help individual Ss to complete the task orally, using the prompts, plan, etc provided. When satisfied that Ss can cope adequately with the task, assign it as written HW.)*

(Suggested answer)

> 14A Dene Crescent
> Ryton
> Tyne & Wear NE40 3RY
>
> 8th November, ...

Dear Gordon,
   Sorry I haven't written for ages, but I have been very busy with all the preparations for my birthday party.
   I have already prepared a few things. I have phoned my friends and I have bought everything I need for the barbecue. I have also borrowed some CDs.
   There are some things I haven't done yet. I haven't ordered a cake yet and I haven't bought a film for my camera.
   Remember, my birthday party is on Saturday 1st December. I hope you can be there!

> Best wishes,
> Bob

Unit 15 - Whatever Will Be, Will Be (pp. 60 - 63)

Objectives

Vocabulary: education; transport; housing; the environment; health; lifestyles
Grammar: "will" for predictions; because; so
Reading: reading for specific information; reading for detailed understanding
Writing: an article predicting what life will be like in the year 2200

1 *(Ask Ss to look at the pictures then read the descriptions aloud. Ss match the descriptions to the pictures while you explain any unknown words.)*

1 C   2 E   3 B   4 A   5 D   6 F

2 *(Ss read the three possible uses of **will**/**won't** and circle the correct one [2c]. Elicit from Ss the tenses used for a [be going to] and b [present continuous]. Also explain that **won't** is the contraction of **will not**.)*

3 *(Read the prompts aloud. Ss make predictions about the future, as in the example.)*

(Suggested answers)

- In my opinion people won't travel by aeroplane. They will travel by spaceship.
- In my opinion people won't only live on Earth. They will also live in colonies on other planets.
- In my opinion people won't live in small houses. They will live in tall buildings made of metal and glass.
- In my opinion people won't only travel to other countries. They will also travel to other planets.

4 a *(Remind Ss of the use of topic sentences [a sentence which starts and summarises a paragraph]. Allow Ss four minutes to read the article and fill in the topic sentences. Check Ss' answers by asking individual Ss to read the article aloud. Explain any unknown words.)*

1 c   2 a   3 b

b *(Allow Ss five minutes to read the article again and answer the questions, then check their answers around the class.)*

1 No, it won't. It will be a lot more fun.
2 They will learn at home with computers.

3 They will use spaceships because space travel will be cheap.
4 They will live in tall buildings made of metal and glass.
5 Because people won't use petrol or gas.
6 Because there will be cures for all diseases.
7 Because robots will do all the boring jobs.
8 The writer believes that life in the year 2200 will be better.
9 In paragraphs 1 and 3.
10 It starts with "In conclusion".

c) *(Copy the table on the board. Explain the headings, then elicit information from Ss and complete it. Ss do the same in their books. Then, Ss talk about the writer's predictions using the notes.)*

Education	children - learn home - computers
Transport	people - use spaceships - visit planets
Housing	people - live - tall buildings made of metal and glass
The Environment	people - not use petrol/gas
Health	there be cures - all diseases
Lifestyles	people have more free time

(Suggested answers)

- People will use spaceships to visit other planets.
- People will live in tall buildings made of metal and glass.
- People won't use petrol or gas.
- There will be cures for all diseases.
- People will have more free time.

STUDY TIP (p. 61)

*(Present the theory in the Study Tip box. Explain that **will** is used in all persons.)*

5 a) *(Explain these words: **long distances, space shuttles, motorbikes, popular, destination**. Allow Ss three minutes to read the text silently and fill in the correct future forms. Ask individual Ss to read the text aloud while you check Ss' answers.)*

1 won't drive   4 will travel   7 will be
2 will drive   5 won't be   8 will also visit
3 won't use   6 will become

b) *(Explain the task to Ss. Ss tick the appropriate boxes. Check Ss' answers, then Ss make sentences using **will** or **won't**.)*

TRANSPORT/TRAVEL	2200
cars that use petrol	✗
electric cars	✔
aeroplanes	✗
space shuttles	✔
motorbikes	✗
bicycles	✔
the moon	✔
other countries	✔

(Suggested answers)

People won't use aeroplanes.
People will travel in space shuttles.
People won't have motorbikes.
People will use bicycles.
People will travel to the moon.
People will travel to other countries.

STUDY TIP (p. 62)

(Present the theory in the Study Tip box and explain/elicit the meaning of any unknown words.)

6 *(Explain the meaning of **optimistic**/**pessimistic**. Individual Ss read aloud items 1 to 7. Explain any unknown vocabulary, then Ss do the exercise. Check Ss' answers around the class.)*

1 O	3 P	5 O	7 P
2 O	4 P	6 P	

7 *(Go through the prompts and explain any unknown vocabulary. Ss, in closed pairs, match the prompts in the two columns. Check Ss' answers, then ask individual Ss to make sentences using **because**. As an extension, Ss can be assigned Ex. 7 as written HW.)*

1 b   2 e   3 a   4 c   5 d

2 People won't swim in the sea because the sea will be polluted.
3 People will live underground because there won't be enough space on Earth.
4 Some animals will disappear because there won't be enough food for them.
5 People will be poorer because there will be fewer jobs.

8 *(Read aloud the causes 1 to 6, then ask individual Ss to read aloud what each person says. Ss match the causes to the effects. Check Ss' answers, then Ss make sentences using **so**. As an extension, Ss can be assigned Ex. 8 as written HW.)*

1 e   2 a   3 d   4 c   5 f   6 b

2 The sea will be polluted, so there won't be any fish.
3 Robots will work as cleaners and builders, so people will have less boring jobs.
4 There will be more cars, so pollution will get worse.
5 People will work twenty hours a week, so people will enjoy more free time.
6 There won't be enough trees, so there won't be enough oxygen.

9 *(Ask Ss to silently read the sentences in the first section of the table (Education). Explain/Elicit the meaning of any unknown vocabulary. Ss match items 1 and 2 in Column A to items a and b in column B. Check Ss' answers, then ask individual Ss to make sentences using **because** or **so**. Do the same with the other sections in the table. Practise with more than two Ss each time.)*

Education

1b Children will learn at home with computers, **so** there won't be any classes.
2a Children won't make any friends **because** they won't go to school.

Transport

1a There will be more cars than people, **so** traffic problems will be worse.
2b There will be more traffic accidents **because** cars will be able to travel faster.

Housing

1b There won't be enough space on Earth, **so** people will build underwater cities.
2a People will live on other planets **because** the air on Earth will be polluted.

The Environment

1b There won't be any fish **because** the seas and rivers will be polluted.
2a The air will be very polluted, **so** people will wear oxygen masks.

Health

1b   There won't be enough food, **so** people will die of hunger.

2a   People will die younger **because** there will be more diseases.

Lifestyles

1a   People who will have jobs, will work longer hours, **so** they will have less free time.

2b   Many people won't be able to find a job **because** companies will use robots instead of people.

WRITING TIP (p. 63)

(Present the theory in the Writing Tip box and ask Ss to check whether the article in Ex.4 conforms to this theory.)

10 *(Remind Ss to use the title, the beginning and ending given and the paragraph plan. Then, assign the task as written HW. Point out that Ss should use only one point of view from each section in Ex. 9.)*

(Suggested answer)

(Para 2)

... Firstly, children will learn at home with computers, so there won't be any classes. Also, there will be more traffic accidents because cars will be able to travel faster. What is more, there won't be enough space on Earth, so people will build underwater cities and the air will be very polluted, so people will wear oxygen masks. Finally, there won't be enough food, so people will die of hunger and people who will have jobs, will work longer hours, so they will have less free time.